Creating Equity-Centered Communities

Creating Equity-Centered Communities

Belonging, Bold Hope, and You

Teresa G. Perkins

BLOOMSBURY ACADEMIC
NEW YORK • LONDON • OXFORD • NEW DELHI • SYDNEY

BLOOMSBURY ACADEMIC

Bloomsbury Publishing Inc, 1359 Broadway, New York, NY 10018, USA
Bloomsbury Publishing Plc, 50 Bedford Square, London, WC1B 3DP, UK
Bloomsbury Publishing Ireland, 29 Earlsfort Terrace, Dublin 2, D02 AY28, Ireland

BLOOMSBURY, BLOOMSBURY ACADEMIC and the Diana logo are trademarks of Bloomsbury Publishing Plc

First published in the United States of America 2018

Copyright © Teresa G. Perkins, 2025

For legal purposes the Acknowledgments on p. vii constitute an extension of this copyright page.

Cover image © iStock.com/Rifqyhsn Design

All rights reserved. No part of this publication may be: i) reproduced or transmitted in any form, electronic or mechanical, including photocopying, recording or by means of any information storage or retrieval system without prior permission in writing from the publishers; or ii) used or reproduced in any way for the training, development or operation of artificial intelligence (AI) technologies, including generative AI technologies. The rights holders expressly reserve this publication from the text and data mining exception as per Article 4(3) of the Digital Single Market Directive (EU) 2019/790.

Bloomsbury Publishing Inc does not have any control over, or responsibility for, any third-party websites referred to or in this book. All internet addresses given in this book were correct at the time of going to press. The author and publisher regret any inconvenience caused if addresses have changed or sites have ceased to exist, but can accept no responsibility for any such changes.

A catalog record for this book is available from the Library of Congress.

ISBN: HB: 978-1-4758-7085-5
PB: 978-1-4758-7086-2
ePDF: 979-8-7651-6027-5
eBook: 978-1-4758-7087-9

Typeset by Deanta Global Publishing Services, Chennai, India
Printed and bound in the United States of America

For product safety related questions contact productsafety@bloomsbury.com.

To find out more about our authors and books visit www.bloomsbury.com and sign up for our newsletters.

Contents

Acknowledgments vii
Preface viii

Introduction 1

Part I Reflection as Momentum 7

1 Self-Reflection: Fuel for Hope-Filled Action 9

2 Which Momentum Are You a Part of? 17

3 Momentum for Transformational Change 31

4 Unity and Human Dynamics 41

5 What Is Missing and What Is Needed? 55

6 Hope Is a Verb 69

7 Community Building Is Capacity Building 81

Part II The Sweet Spot of Belonging and Hope 91

8 The People-Centered Promise 93

9 The Essentialness of Belonging 105

10 Showing Up with Hope 113

11 When Belonging and Hope Coexist: The Sweet Spot of Equity-Centered Communities 121

12 Hope Anyway 129

Bibliography 135
About the Author 139

Acknowledgments

This book would not have moved from a whispered hope to reality without a lot of people believing in me. I am incredibly grateful for this "yes" from Bloomsbury Publishing and for the steady support from April Snider at Bloomsbury.

Officially, this research and writing spanned nearly two years; in reality, I have been holding on to hope and belonging as long as I can remember. I am grateful for each student I have been fortunate enough to learn and grow with over the last thirty plus years.

Authentic connection, *the sweet spot of hope and belonging*, has been part of my journey because of my friends and colleagues who show up every day with a servant's heart and disposition for our calling, thank you for inspiring me.

My deepest gratitude to the people who mean the most to me, my family. Todd, my life is infinitely better because you are mine and I am yours. Thank you to the ones who supply the light and love in my world, you are my heart: *Emily, Lydia, Adam, Eli, Riley, Kyle, and Hayden*.

To the one who taught me to hope, my mama, always in my heart.

Preface

In the mid-1970s, the metro school district I attended as an elementary student in the US Midwest faced a legal challenge to uphold *Brown v. Board of Ed*,[1] in the action of *United States v. School District of Omaha*.[2] The results of the lawsuit rippled to my world in the faded red brick elementary school building located in a predominantly white, working-class neighborhood. The school district's response included an integration plan of busing certain grade levels of students in elementary school to one side of the city and other grade levels of elementary students to another side of the city.

Forty-five years later, I vividly remember the image of my third-grade teacher, a respected and popular white female, standing in front of the class, tears running down her face, telling the rows of white students quietly staring back that "they" were "making" her teach on the "other side of town." Whatever words the visibly shaken veteran teacher went on to use detailing the legal circumstances of the decision were lost on nine-year-old me.

What was not lost on me as I sat among neighborhood friends in a traditional classroom, windows open with the spring breeze circulating through the desks neatly in rows, walls brightly decorated with the cursive alphabet lining one side of the chalkboard, and pictures of all the white male presidents lining the other side of the board, was the sadness and grief enveloping the space. The feeling of something negative and sad being done to my teacher—seemingly all based on race, geography, and humanness—was tinged with fear and uncertainty. This emotion-filled announcement by someone I trusted was my formal introduction to forced communities.

Missing from most of the early desegregation conversations I was privy to in my childhood were elements of equity-centered, hope-filled possibilities that, today I like to believe, were some of the intentions of the mandates. The divisiveness and uncertainty of the hallway chatter between teachers and students alike, and the at-home conversations with small head shakes while watching the local evening news, were actually symptoms of a system under well-deserved scrutiny, as much as those moments were about necessary change.

Only the decision-makers "at the table" know the details and intentionality behind the decisions made in the room. Who is at the table? Who decides? How do the decision-makers truly "know" multiple perspectives and lived experiences are not only represented and will also benefit from the decisions? How often do you, personally and professionally, consider the "Who is at the table?" question? The continuous improvement models available from State Departments of Education and educational researchers call for monitoring and evaluating to determine effectiveness. The process of systems-checking to support continuous improvement also applies to individuals, to us, each of us, regardless of title or role within the organization.

Building intentional systems of equity and hope-filled purpose is, at times, just as messy as dismantling inequitable systems. Construction is messy and so is deconstruction. Throughout this book, you are encouraged to self-assess your individual role (real or potential) in the messiness of creating communities of belonging and hope. If you think the messiness leads to transforming places and systems, let that possibility fuel you. Choose to build together, in community.

In early 2019, as an assistant professor at a small liberal arts university in the same city as the neatly rowed classroom from decades ago, I started meeting with graduate students seeking a master's degree in educational leadership. Many of those conversations with teacher leaders and school leaders from across the city were tinged with confusion and hesitation. People openly shared confusion and uncertainty about the next, right steps for purposeful, passionate educators, focused on how to create inclusive communities, *despite* the political-social noise of the day . . . or maybe *because of* the noise.

Some of the conversations and intellectual exchanges I experienced with graduate-level students, who are also full-time educational practitioners, are so laced with the power of hope and the possibilities existing around equity-centered communities of belonging that I refer to some of these students as "Hope Makers."

The Hope Makers, who show up with hope-filled armor securely in place, regularly find themselves in spaces and environments at times filled with stress and an uncertain future. Yet, guided by dispositions rooted in hope, these individuals know and understand the difference between wishful thinking and hope-filled, purpose-driven action.

The real and raw conversations among people of goodwill and educators from a variety of school locations, with a variety of experiences, representing demographics from across the world co-mingle with many of the same components from my third-grade, mid-1970s classroom: race, geography, and humanness.

The complicity of time is one element in the underpinnings of systems perpetuating and maintaining human inequity. What and who are thriving because of the partnership between silence and trading on time? Throughout this work, notice the various timestamps connecting the journey toward creating equity-centered communities of belonging and hope. Who is asking whom to wait? Who is leveraging time and for what purpose? Is time weaponized or wielded as an absolvent? The complicity of time is unpacked throughout this book, with cues for reflection along the way.

This is not just another book about equity. Personal and systematic transformation start here. If our common goals include building relationships, increasing personal capacity, recognizing, and removing systemic inequities, we are required to push past haphazard acts of improvement and policies that divide rather than unify.

The frameworks and processes in this book provide prompts, conversation starters, and reflective activities aimed to increase understanding and personal application of hope-filled next steps. Purposeful next steps toward achieving connections and creating equity-centered communities of belonging begin with each one of us.

As learning leaders, regardless of current position, accept the cultural proficiency call to create equity-centered, inclusive communities of belonging and hope. The work begins with each individual's willingness to look inside. Read the first sentence of this paragraph again; this time insert the word "people" in place of "learning leaders."

The ability to look inside with the purposeful intent to understand the "why" behind beliefs, feelings, and actions is the real-world responsibility for each of us, regardless of where we live and work. Shared lived experiences ought not to be a prerequisite to sharing goals for a better tomorrow. You have likely heard a variation of the expression *it does not have to happen to you for it to matter to you.*

The structure and components of conceptual frameworks included in this book are intended to scaffold and broaden the understanding of personal reflection. Self-reflection, through personal assessment, coupled with intentional vocabulary, creates a common language for readers to apply in personal and community settings. Serving as a reflective practitioner with a robust lens of equity, diversity, and inclusion is not bound to a specific or titled position.

How do people first identify bias in self, and then systems, working together to change, disrupt, and/or rebuild systems? Notice the preceding question starts with self. A reflective practitioner's first step is uncovering and exploring personally held biases. The foundational roots in communities of belonging and hope take hold in knowing and understanding that each lived experience is valuable for the whole.

Invested readers gain a stronger knowledge base of authentic culturally proficient leadership practices and systems through self-assessment, reflection, and vocabulary acquisition, while identifying the skills and dispositions necessary to create communities of belonging and hope. This book explores and defines culturally proficient academic vocabulary, including equity, diversity, biases, micro and macro aggressions, and social constructs, all while aiming to build a solid foundation of systemic and systematic support for people who are marginalized[2] and minoritized (Souto-Manning et al., 2018). Through authentic community building, rooted in belonging and hope, we share an unwavering commitment to the multi-dimensions of humanity. Each time phrases like *building a solid foundation* are used throughout this book, consider those words to signal an invitation and opportunities to create calls to action and next steps.

What is not contained within the pages of this book is a series of rubrics with clear-cut pathways of proficiency measures to achieve every nuance of human connection through shared values and vision. Though the lifelong learner and educator in me appreciates a well-designed system of monitoring and evaluating progress toward goals, we cannot intellectualize ourselves into creating equity-centered communities. Just as it is improbable to talk ourselves into believing we belong somewhere when, at best, we merely fit in.

My personal discovery around the power of hope and belonging started as a young girl, safeguarded by a mom whose essence and existence were held together by hope. I am not exactly sure when I realized my first teacher and role model of a hope-filled life was my mama; though I do know I was, unfortunately, well into adulthood.

Are you reading this book because your curiosity about the connective tissue of reflection, belonging, and hope already exists, or because in one space or another you have been moved to the edges and experienced faux inclusion? Maybe your "why" for reading lives in the spaces somewhere inside or outside those two reasons. Whatever the catalyst for reading a book about belonging and hope, I encourage you to own the next steps for yourself.

Each step forward with a framed understanding, ownership, and laser-like intention on authentic inclusion creates spaces and places for communities of belonging and hope.

How we spend our time equals our purpose.

The quickly swinging pendulum of socio-political attitudes around inclusive communities, equity initiatives, and educational policy is dizzying at times. A day-to-day pulse check on the priorities of the dominant culture decision-makers seems necessary. At the final stages of editing this book in March 2024, the United States House of Representatives Office of Diversity and Inclusion was dissolved. Formed just four years prior, its purpose and stated mission highlighted the creation of a congressional workforce more reflective of the country. The dissolution of the Office of Diversity and Inclusion at the highest governing body in the Nation sends a message, regardless of political affiliation. Systems are built intentionally, and systems are also dismantled intentionally.

Throughout the writing and research for this book, I realized checking-in with my whiteness had to be one of my requisites. A colleague, mentor, and trusted confidant once said to me, "I don't want to walk into a room where my blackness doesn't show up first." Because of the known, unknown, and unearned advantages of whiteness, I do not hold the same sentiment about my racial identity when I "show up."

I am fully aware the previous sentence is fodder for some to turn away from this writing and offers fuel for others. I am responsible for naming my own truth, based on my life experiences, a shared responsibility for each of us if an authentic community grounded in belonging is the goal.

A straightforward disclaimer is offered at the outset of this book: the personal and collective work of intentional identification, uncovering and discovering connections, learning, and application toward creating equity-centered communities of belonging and hope is not easy. This focused work does not create soft landing spots for people and groups accustomed to living comfortably in the middle—even if someone is aware of the unearned privileges associated with holding space at the center.

Consider this book a practical toolkit and companion for the heart and hard work you are doing around self-reflection. The words, concepts, and provocations offered in this writing are meant to meet each reader in the moment, exactly as you are today. Meeting in the moment is sometimes complicated, raw, and unsteady . . . because we are humans. The human experience may be messy and can be trying.

The human experience is also joyful. It turns out the road to joy is complicated and probably includes unpredicted obstacles . . . and the journey is still worth it. My hope for you, for each of us, is we choose to grow together, not apart.

Notes

1. Considered a landmark 1954 US Supreme Court case ruling racial segregation in schools was unconstitutional. The unanimous decision overturned the 1896 "separate but equal" ruling of *Plessy v. Ferguson* case (archives.gov).
2. In this book, terms such as "marginalized" and "minoritized" are used to name a truth not always acknowledged by the dominant white culture. Similarly, when I write "people of color" it is not my intention to simplify or add to the erasure of people and individuals. The social construct of race, created to divide and categorize, is woven together with the power of the language we speak to and about each other. The intended impact of my word choice is framed in respect and honor; I am a woman who is white, who begins each day hoping to be better and daring to do better than the day before.

Introduction

Suggestions for Reading

- Have a writing utensil handy, even if you are not one who typically writes in the book.
- Lean into the spaces throughout this book intentionally designed to Pause and Process, and practice self-reflection, even if you would rather not, maybe especially if you would rather not.
- Consider your individual role and responsibility within each community you hold membership.
- Ask yourself questions while you read and reflect; notice what you are curious about and what you are certain about.
- Notice when curiosity comes before judgment, and vice versa.
- Accept the calls to action you feel stirring inside, even if the first step is a small one; all forward steps are moving in the desired direction.
- Own the truth about disposition over position. Often, what is on the inside predicts more about an individual's ability to create spaces for belonging and hope than the title of the position. For instance, education is full of leaders, which is a strength of the profession. Titles and positions do not make someone a leader, disposition does.
- Do not be afraid to uncover missed opportunities or past failures. Productive failure is the often unnoticed byproduct of attempts at progress. The image of a mountain climber comes to mind. Of course, climbing can be difficult. Even the most seasoned climber slips and falls occasionally. The climbers who stand back up, shake off the stumble, and with a knee brush take another step are the ones leading the way. Keep climbing. Your "future self" is counting on you to forge pathways of possibility built with hope . . . not just for yourself but for the people with you today and the ones who will come after you.
- Throughout the book, there are few recurring features strategically placed to keep you *in the work* of growing as a reflective thinker

and processor—Chapter Takeaways end each chapter with a few summary sentences and reflective questions to support your personal processing. Prompts for hands-on personal inquiry engagement are built-in throughout the book and include these types of exercises:

- Pause and Process
- The Four Stages of Learning©
- The Reflective Process

At a Glance: The Words We Use

Language is powerful. When you are able to name a thing, it moves out of the realm of mystery into concreteness.

Hammond (2015, 5)

Establishing working definitions of commonly used terms in this book creates a foundation for the research, thought threads, and activities within. Common language and understanding of word choice bind community members together without potentially avoidable communication barriers. Communication creates opportunities for successful or stressful interactions.

Simply put, communication fuels success or stress. Mutual understanding and working definitions of words connect us to each other and experiences. We are hardwired to make connections and add meaning to words and ideas.

The reflexive truth about human nature is we reach for word meanings and associations closest to us, based on our lived experiences. For example, when I come across the word "nurse" in conversation or reading, my working definition is automatically connected to the skilled and compassionate oncology healthcare providers who cared for my mom during the last two years of her life. I know the generic definition of "nurse" well enough; however, my reflexive first touch of the word is rooted in my lived experiences.

When you come across the words "teacher" or "doctor" or "friend" what is your automatic working definition? Without being able to hear your response, I am willing to guess you included an association based on your lived experiences, positive and/or negative.

For each of the words defined in this section, a longer, more scholarly definition could most certainly be provided. Rather than supplying a solely academic meaning, I intentionally chose to offer accessible and actionable working definitions. Over thirty years ago, my undergraduate, 400-level Linguistics course professor Dr. Larry Andrews reminded the class over and over that the most effective communication is that which is accessible to as many people as possible.

Throughout the book, if you come across a definition or example of a word/concept that expands your thinking, understanding, and working definition, I hope you stop and note (in a system that works best for you) the additional layers of meaning. Each time we *choose* to *own* new learning, we create potential pathways for deeper reflection and application. The topic of creating equity-centered communities of belonging and hope, deeper understanding, and application by one person is momentum forward for the rest of us.

Working Definitions

accountability—the owned responsibility connected to abilities and capabilities.

barriers—block the entrance to community membership and inclusion.

belonging—a positively held sense of membership and essentialness to the group; when *who* you are and who *you* are the very fibers in the fabric of the community.

bias—predetermined allegiance against an individual or group based on unjust criteria.

unconscious or subconscious bias—predetermined judgments held largely without a degree of awareness by the holder.

conscious bias—known judgments by an individual or group

confirmation or desire bias—seeking information or affirmation to support a personally held belief, idea, or understanding

implicit bias—the beliefs and understandings that inform one's opinions on a topic, individual, or group.

call to action—named next step, including specifics around measures of success and progress toward the goal; this is an identified and definable action, not a hypothetical or vague outcome.

change demanders—individuals who no longer accept systemic oppression, demonstrated by voice and meaningful, measurable actions.

co-conspirator—individual who takes action in opportunities and environments to create equity-centered realities for all, leveraging privilege to cause action beyond allyship or partnership. One of the strongest descriptions of the co-conspirator mindset I am aware of is part of Dr. Bettina Love's C-SPAN interview in April 2019.

cognitively flexible—the will and capability to demonstrate curiosity, including the willingness to learn and adjust prior knowledge and understanding based on new (to you) information, concepts, ideas, or possibilities.

cognitively closed—a limited and limiting "thought state"; the inability to accept or process the possibility of information, concepts, ideas, or possibilities outside of one's lived experiences or current understanding.

community—a group of individuals with intersecting humanity-based interests, selectively linked by self- and/or assigned membership by other individuals or groups.

disposition—individual characteristics and qualities held within and outwardly demonstrated, regardless of position or role assignment within a community.

diversity—the composition of a variety of differences, unlimited.

efficacy—level of effectiveness and achievement toward identified and intended results.

ethical tension—the feeling caused by existing in the space between knowing what the next right step is and actually taking the next right step.

equity—the value focusing on the same levels of high achievement for each person, without the existence of dominant or marginalized and minoritized classifications.

hope—a value-centered principle, disciplined thinking, and way of believing, with roots in positive perseverance and disposition.

inclusive language—more word choice options to describe lived experiences.

limiting language—narrow word choice options, keeping and containing lived experiences in a box, generalized and perpetuating stereotypes and biases.

macro-aggression—the overt use of words or actions to intentionally assert dominance over a person or group.

micro-aggression—the subtle use of words or actions to claim dominance over a person or group, consciously/unconsciously.

privileges—earned or unearned advantages held by some members of the group, and not others.

reflection—the personal process of interrogating beliefs, understanding, and knowledge of one's circumstances, experiences, perceptions, and realities.

social constructs—systems developed by people to classify and group others based on appearances, most often to create hierarchical and arbitrary divisions among humanity.

systemic—infused and part of the entire system.

systems—step by step structures creating processes

virtue signaling—the public-facing expression of supporting equity, inclusion, and justice without meaningful actions. Virtue signaling is performative, not substantive, and attached to the inclusion illusion.

"Language matters. It's the raw material of the story, it changes how we feel about ourselves and others, and it's a portal to connection" (Brown 2022, 235).

Part I
Reflection as Momentum

1 Self-Reflection
Fuel for Hope-Filled Action

In early 2023, I was invited to talk about the concepts of cultural proficiency through the connecting elements of reflection and forward movement with a graduate-level leadership class focused on diversity, equity, and inclusion. As I facilitated a conversation about equity-centered systems, a mid-twenties, third-year teacher in the class asked, "When are we going to stop talking about equity and actually do something?"

The early educator earning a master's degree in educational leadership went on to describe a nearly combustible community where divisions run deep, and regular news reports of violence and social unrest have a numbing effect. The silent nods from some of the other graduate students added confirmation to the statements, as others mumbled, "yes" in agreement to the atmosphere and description.

When are "we" going to stop talking about equity and do something? Indeed. The automatic response I offered the graduate student was, "Now. Yesterday. Last week. Four decades ago. What are we waiting for?" With my response in question form, I might also add a truth.

Not all individuals and communities are waiting for systems to be dismantled or seeking opportunities to build a new way forward.

Not all people are waiting. Some individuals, groups, and organizations continue to support the firmly entrenched systems, intentionally or otherwise. And still, other community members are waiting for someone else to lead, through a more passive *followers'* mindset.

Of course, the good news, the hope-filled truth is, not everyone is willing to wait either. By asking the question during the graduate-level leadership class, laced with frustration and steeped in readiness, that third-year educator represented hope and action. Why hope? The third-year teacher, graduate student, brave enough to verbalize impatience in question form was a white, blue-eyed, blonde-haired, cisgender male, teaching in a Midwest middle school. These outward-facing descriptors are offered to confirm another truth: hope and action have many faces.

When the twenty-year-old pre-med undergrad female student of color completed McIntosh's White Privilege Survey during a University-wide Rev. Dr. Martin Luther King, Jr. presentation I was leading, she looked up and asked a room of mostly white, middle-aged academics, "So, now that I know I scored a 3 out of 130, what happens next?" This also represents hope and action. Her score, she said, did not surprise her. I scanned the room filled with titled leaders, predominantly white, from across the community and wondered how her question landed. Would the people in the room who scored a perfect 130/130 be spurred to change systems, environments, or policies that provided a comfortable place to stand? What sparks curiosity in people whose vantage points are supported by the status quo? The individuals who choose to lean in and understand *where* they are and where *they* are within various communities embody hope and action. Asking questions represents potential progress. Look around, notice who is asking questions, and what are the questions being asked?

It is likely more individuals are asking the "when" and "how" questions than is reflected in the noisy environments highlighted on the news and social media feeds. People of goodwill grab hold of the momentum created by fellow questioners within communities and intentionally leverage the fuel of hope-filled purpose to cause action. At times, individuals self-reflect because of a movement, and sometimes self-reflection causes a movement.

In the two years since researching and authoring this book began, I have spoken on the topics of creating communities rooted in equity, belonging, and hope with hundreds of community leaders, educators, and parents/guardians from across the United States and around the world. The political landscape remains scattered with ideological and belief divides; so too remains the truth that hope-filled, purpose-driven people keep showing up.

Purposeful, systematic, and intentional reflection is a personal fact-checking system for cultivating hope and pinpointing places in daily experiences bolstered by your personally defined mission and purpose. At the most authentic and invested state, self-reflection is the connective tissue binding people together who choose to build inclusive communities of belonging and hope.

Through the process of individual reflection, the intentional self-exploration of personal and systemic barriers is uncovered, or at least, the possibility exists to identify barriers. What are the barriers you navigate around or through? What barriers exist you (or another) cannot cross?

During self-reflection, the vulnerable and raw work of personal discovery occurs for each of us on a continuum of individual development. This personal discovery is the first step in moving forward and identifying obstacles for yourself and others. The "when," "how," and "who" questions take hold and gain momentum in self-reflection.

Defining moments of *who* we are and who *we* are as individuals emerge when self-reflection becomes part of a positive routine, an intentional habit. Exploring the pieces of our individual, daily interactions with the systematic reflective process identified in this book offers the possibility of bringing the tensions and testaments of individual human experiences to the surface.

The reflection framework offered in this book is anchored to a series of questions developed to support and guide the reflective process. The layers of learning questions are designed as prompts and personal thought-builders.

The Four Stages of Learning©:

- What am I learning?
    - What am I relearning?
        - What am I unlearning
            - What am I resisting learning?

Individuals willing to investigate their own beliefs, values, practices, and experiences create space and opportunity to expand personal knowledge and understanding, which happen to be the precursors to forward personal momentum.

An intended outcome of your investment within the pages of this book is self-reflection as a precursor to self-inquiry. Consider this an invitation to see and own the tools of self-reflection connected to growth. Self-reflection leads to knowing and understanding *who you are* outside of who the world tells you to be.

Specific, measurable calls to action are grounded in unpacking the four reflective questions pinned to the Four Stages of Learning© progression. When individuals are open to receiving new information on existing knowledge and understanding, consciously or unconsciously gained, cognitive flexibility is leveraged; this is part of the heart and hard work of humanity.

Among a reflective practitioner's tools are desire and curiosity, including the willingness to learn and adjust previously held knowledge and understanding based on new levels of information, concepts, ideas, or possibilities. Curiosity is fueled by willingness and capability, read another way as Will and Skill.

The grounded theory of self-assessment through reflective practices is framed within the mindset around words educators commonly refer to as lifelong learning. The unraveling of people's individual and collective interactions begins with a personal willingness to start with self. The personal consideration of a lifelong learner mindset is the intentional reflection on topics already known about in a way that allows new information to be received, along with new data which might be contrary, and in some cases is contrary, to what is already believed to be known.

There is a human instinct to resist ideas, ideals, or concepts contrary to what is or was previously known as accurate. Because this humanistic resistance exists almost at the level of self-preservation (insert dangers like fire or flood; when we are aware of the potential of these dangers, we resist and actively work against the occurrence of circumstances netting such results), developing a system for recognizing when your resistance mindset is taking over and controlling your next steps is a foundational piece for self-reflection.

My natural researcher mindset seeks themes, trends, and opportunities to analyze situations with data, both offered and sought. The two-year process of researching, collecting empirical data, and drafting this book included consuming as much information, both current and historical, on the topics of self-reflection, community building, belonging, and hope. Immersion in the concepts and research is one way of providing a thorough and developed resource. Routine reminders to meet the reader, meet you, right where you are today also required me to share where I am today with you.

The reciprocity of sharing real and raw parts of ourselves with others we are in a community with comes with a prerequisite to building and sustaining an equity-centered community. Each of us must *first* look inside with the genuine goal of more fully understanding who we are and how we show up in the community with others. In community building, individuals come together, not just with the best and brightest parts available, but also with the real and gritty pieces of humanity offered as examples of growth and learning.

Throughout this book, firsthand experiences are offered to meet you in the moment, even when the personal experiences represent underdeveloped times in the journey, times when the mark was entirely missed. Throughout life have you consistently chosen to fail forward? The messy, complicated, underdeveloped parts of a life story include experiences where the target was miserably missed and still, despite failing, people dig in their heels. Sometimes, we hold our ground so long, only to look around to see the people we are standing with and discover misalignment.

Mission misalignment is not neat and tidy. Consider personal mission misalignment as the times and instances when people do not share goals for community building; it is in those situations when belonging is missing. Throughout life, during instances of failure, lean hard into reflection, even when authentically reflecting is the last thing you want to be doing. Sometimes the greatest opportunity for learning and growth happens at the feet of failure.

The reflective process supported by the Four Stages of Learning© does not ask anyone to disregard previous learning or lived experiences. In fact, lean into and own your previous learning. Understanding what you know, the source of that knowledge, and information gaps serves as the foundational steps for moving forward as a reflective practitioner.

Imagine your learning, or more directly stated, what you "know," on any given topic as something tangible, something examinable under a metaphorical microscope. Even if you have not previously considered yourself a researcher, as you read and respond to the reflective prompts in this book, you are in fact a researcher of sorts. You are the researcher of *who* you are, the ideas and beliefs you hold, along with your community memberships.

Researchers, by definition, are seekers. Researchers are curious and focus on answering in-depth questions on the topic at hand. Consider this your invitation to seek to know and understand more—more about *who* you are and who *you* are, and more about the people you serve, support, and influence, regardless of assigned role(s).

The circumstances and systems shaping your individual knowing and understanding may have been built on uneven levels of development and purposes. How will you know what shaped and shapes what you know without committing to regularly questioning, noting, and owning actions, understandings, and beliefs? Commit and recommit. Intentional self-reflection creates opportunities to uncover and discover more learning on a topic.

Consider the *sage on the stage* mindset related to equity-centered communities of belonging and hope, where authentic connection is the glue. In this case, the *sage* analogy depicts individuals who spend a significant amount of time certain they are the people with most of the answers, holding little space for questions or curiosity about the effects of their own and others' decisions and systems' results.

When someone is cognitively closed, possessing a limited and limiting ability to accept or process even the possibility of information, concepts, or ideas outside their individually lived experiences or current understanding, personally held biases flourish. The *sage* way of being represents real and potential limitations, or distinct boundary lines, in new knowledge acquisition.

The subtlety of standing in the shade of intellectualization shields the *sage* from acknowledging a need for personal growth or recognizing overt systemic inequities. Research from a distance is not solution-oriented; it is not possible to research your way out of a blind spot.

The invitation for you to process through the Four Stages of Learning© does not diminish your personally held expertise; rather, lean into the truth there is not a ceiling for learning. When is a topic exhausted in the reflective process? The concise answer for when a topic ceases to exist as a thought thread for further reflection is when the topic no longer exists.

Cognitive flexibility engages a reflective muscle, at times requiring personal risk-taking to uncover hidden biases and blind spots. Cognitively flexible people are willing to do the *inside work* even when focusing more on what is happening on the outside is less of a personal lift. The Four Stages of Learning© encourages curiosity, supported by a willingness to learn and adjust prior knowledge and understanding based on new (to you) information, concepts, ideas, or possibilities.

Self-assessment and reflection are wrapped around seeking and curiosity—thoughtfully curious about yourself. When we are curious about a topic, seeking to know more, at a deeper level of understanding, is a natural byproduct.

Self-reflection is an authentically inward process, choosing to come face to face with yourself. The four separate components of the Reflective Process offered in this book aim for personal growth through knowing and owning *where* you stand and *why*. The amount of personal investment in fully developing each component of the Reflective Process directly determines your magnitude of growth. Choose to go a little deeper than a surface-level glimpse at your *why*, or the routine, automatic response automatically given.

Chapter Takeaways

Identifying personal and systemic reflective topics means you are willing to peel back the layers and discern why this is an "unpacking topic," aka self-discovery. Who and what do you value? How are your values demonstrated? What are the connections and disconnects to your personally held beliefs?

First, tell your individual truth and then reconcile currently known truths with hope-filled, purposeful calls to action. Who do you aspire to be, what are some possible pathways, and who will go with you?

2 Which Momentum Are You a Part of?

Going alone on this personal journey of self-assessment and reflection is optional; not going at all is not an option. Authenticity in true community is based on knowing and believing in lived experiences, even when, especially when, someone's life experiences are vastly different from any of yours.

Increasing self-awareness requires truth-telling. Tell yourself the truth about who you are, rather than the surface definition. The momentum of individuals and communities intentionally seeking to interrupt, disrupt, and dismantle systemic barriers is fueled by self-assessment and reflection.

American author James Baldwin (1962) remarked how often people are afraid to tell the truth because trusting the story one is telling requires a look inside self.

At times, the reflexive, unconscious act is to create desired stories; creating desired personal narratives, rather than admitting to the underdeveloped or hidden parts of self is a comfortable place to stand. In these times, the personal narratives we write, tell, and believe are more often rooted in aspirations of who we want to be. "Not everything that is faced can be changed, but nothing can be changed until it is faced" (Baldwin 1962).

Aspiration is potential fuel, as long as the ideas of "someday" and "when the time is right" do not become the fallback response to "why not now?" So, how does an individual turn closely held aspirational beliefs into a daily walk? By dealing with, and understanding, what the unspoken words might be hiding and what those same words reveal. Naming, owning, and aiming who you are today and who you will be tomorrow is developed through the intentional practice of self-reflection.

Dismantling inequitable systems amidst political-social noise and naming unjust social constructs is a responsibility we each own. The collective forward movement of everyone within an organization creates momentum. So, too, does the backward slide of exclusionary practices and policies. Which momentum are you a part of? If you are in the organization, you are part of the movement. The ethical mandate to disrupt pedagogically inequitable and exclusive systems is now. How do you know if you are part of the forward momentum or creating an unintended or intended roadblock? Knowing your role(s) within any given group or community begins with self-reflection.

As a graduate studies professor, I have asked hundreds of prospective students, who also happen to be full-time educators (i.e., classroom teachers, instructional facilitators, school psychologists), to share their individual working definitions of diversity, equity, and inclusion. A common response from well-meaning individuals includes, "There is not a lot of diversity where I am; I do not have much experience with diversity."

When "diversity" is a term used to describe someone else, or a component of another person's identity, the door to *othering* is opened a little wider. Dominant culture thinking and behaving often includes oversimplifying the definition of diversity to race and ethnicity. In truth, diversity's definition is as wide as each human characteristic.

The limiting and limited views existing in and out of our personal understanding of equity, diversity, and inclusion are starting points on the continuum of development of cultural proficiency. This is the point where Will and Skill meet to deepen capacity and understanding. Reflection begins here; or rather, this is potentially where reflection begins for those who are willing to look inside, committing to capacity building.

Equity is not an item on the shelf, dusted off and donated when the mood strikes, like a philanthropic event. *Equity is a value.* Zeroing in on what you tell yourself, consciously or otherwise, about people who appear different or identify differently than you, is part of your personal narrative. Your personal narrative outlines who is valuable or to what degree of value you hold for the differences between individuals and groups. How do you assess and assign a person's role within a community or the value you hold for the person's role based on differences, real or perceived?

When a person is not wholly valued, it is unrealistic for a workplace, neighborhood, school, or social setting to expect the person to fully engage, perform at their highest capabilities, and openly trust. Unrealistic, and yet, that is exactly what happens every day in cities, communities, businesses, and educational settings.

The messages, overtly and covertly, sent through thinly veiled policies and procedures exclude dimensions of diversity, shaping and defining who each of us are as humans. Socialization teaches us to believe personal value is based on how much our individual intersections of identities are sought after and amplified.

Throughout this book, notice the unpredictable arrangements of the three words: "equity," "inclusion," and "diversity." This is not an editing mistake or inconsistent writing. The choice to avoid the common acronym DEI and the almost rote, rhythmically spoken pattern of diversity, equity, and inclusion is an intentional reminder and reimagining of our individual roles within each of the words. For some of us, realizing the robust definition each of the three words holds emphasizes the equity-centered value of humanness.

To engage in or even discuss efforts prioritizing the value of equity in the United States as this research and writing concludes in 2024 requires acknowledging the polarization occurring across the United States at the mere mention of diversity, inclusion, and equity. The socio-political divisiveness surrounding initiatives falling under the banner of DEI became weaponized and, at least in part, resulted in entire commercial, governmental, and educational institutions disbanding and defunding departments focused on equity, inclusion, and diversity efforts.[1]

Culturally proficient leadership is not a set of glasses someone chooses to put on at certain times of the day or when doing so is convenient. Cultural proficiency is not achieved by looking at the clock each Tuesday afternoon and thinking, "this is my regularly scheduled time to create inclusive communities of belonging and hope." Rather, the melodic tempo of hope-filled, purposeful steps is the consistent background sound toward culturally proficient development. The individual steps each of us take, and do not take, directly reflect personal missions, values, and beliefs, in much the same way systems and spaces hold missions and visions at the root of the work, or not.

The floodgates of purposeful, positive momentum among people of goodwill are thrown open when each of us is courageous enough to uncover and discover personally held biases, known and unknown. Systems and processes cannot be changed without first making space to know and understand personally held ideas, values, and beliefs.

Throughout this book, the case is made, provides evidence for, and invites you into the power of self-reflection. This book offers a solid foundation of the first step, and the next steps, for individuals and organizations committing to the heart and hard work of intentionally creating equity-centered communities of belonging and hope. Personal reflection breaks down barriers, builds on-ramps to learning, and increases self-confidence.

To be yourself in a world that is constantly trying to make you something else is the greatest accomplishment (Emerson 1841, 52).[2]

Books written decades ago offered landscapes of possibilities where people came together through the collective efficacy lens of creating community, and yet still today some are asking *How*? *For whom*? and *when*? The answers lie in the often-overlooked necessity of intentionally carving out space and systems for individuals to begin the reflective practices and interpersonal work of owning unconscious bias supported by social constructs.

Knowing systems are netting the exact results the structures were created to produce, clear points for systemic dismantling are revealed. Without the awareness that inequitable systems exist and are thriving, moving forward with an equity-centered vision in a systematic way is improbable and unlikely.

During 2022–4 as this book was written, I was part of conversations and professional interactions with some individuals who did not demonstrate even a slight awareness of the limiting social constructs baked into daily lives and organizational systems. For instance, in a higher education curriculum planning conversation with colleagues in preparation for Black History Month, a seasoned teacher and leader of four decades reminded the group, with seeming dismay, "not everyone believes there are unjust systems based on race, ethnicity and culture."

She continued by detailing a recent meeting involving district-level leaders from multiple school settings across the Midwest who agreed with proposed state legislation to remove equity, diversity, and inclusion initiatives from PK-12 school requirements. Denying the existence of systemically unjust organizational operations is an example of privilege rooted in white-centered systems and the existence of baked-in benefits.

During another professional conversation about including the word "race" among the named dimensions of diversity, a group of higher education staff and faculty could not immediately agree. Even after a respected group member and person of color explained race does not fall under the same changing categorical definitions as other identities, such as gender, religion, and language, the predominantly white group of people could not reach a consensus on the value of including the word "race" as part of a definition of diversity—in the year 2023, among educated adults, in an academic setting.

In conversations around dimensions of diversity especially, listening for what you disagree with instead of what you agree with is a defensive posture, not one open to new learning. The closed, binary way of thinking about the multitude of human differences sounds like, "I'm right, and that is wrong," leaving little room for curiosity or opportunities to know more/differently through seeking others' perspectives.

As we begin to lean into reflective practices around identification of self, others, and community affiliations, this is a natural place in the work to (re)establish common working definitions around three identifying traits generally associated with human experiences. The meaning and use of the terms "race," "ethnicity," and "nationality" are sometimes clearly and aptly applied, while other times the definitions are blurred together, inadvertently or intentionally.

The American Association of Physical Anthropologists Statement on Race and Racism (2019, 400) reports race "does not have its roots in biological reality . . . over the last five centuries race has become a social reality." Further scientific evidence to counter what some people view as racial differences, the AAPA reminds us 99.9 percent of human DNA is shared and physical attributes (i.e., skin color, hair type, facial features) are not DNA variants. In other words, biological differences are not associated with assigned racial groupings and are societal realities constructed in political, social, and legal systems leveraged to benefit some and disadvantage others.

Ethnicity refers to a person or group's ancestry, generally categorized by geographical locations and cultural distinctions (i.e., food, dress, and religious practices). In a book focused on belonging and equity-centered communities, pointing to the privilege of knowing or being aware of one's ethnicity is a given. The predominantly white privilege in the United States of knowing or having access to ancestral roots is not necessarily an option for descendants of people who were captured and enslaved.

In the late 1990s and early 2000s, the market and ability to find one's ancestral background grew out of genealogical websites designed to provide search features to determine family lineage. With some industry reports touting that over 26 million people accessed at-home ancestry tests by 2019, the compelling drive to know oneself has a few possible pathways of discovery for people able to access and afford the available consumer options.

Nationality identifies the nation/country of origin and/or naturalization. For example, someone born in the United States of America who immigrated to

Spain seeking citizenship might respond to a nationality inquiry as both an American and a Spaniard.

Reflect on what you know and believe about yourself in connection to three dimensions of diversity: race, ethnicity, and nationality. Apply the three identifiers for yourself, if you have the information and are able:

Race: _____

Ethnicity: _____

Nationality: _____

As you applied the three dimensions of diversity for yourself, what were some of your initial thoughts? Is the activity challenging for you? How often have you considered the responses to these three layers of human reality?

When a person moves in and out of daily interactions with little to no consideration of how race, or ethnicity, or gender, or class, or sexuality, and identities around religion/spirituality are influencing interactions with others, that is a privileged position. Identifying the source and ongoing suppliers of unearned advantages precedes knowing how to leverage those same privileges to lessen and remove the negative "ists" systems, that is, racist, sexist, ableist.

Each of us are ancestors in the making. If hearing the word "privilege" attached to your personally held identities elicits feelings tinged with guilt, discomfort, or defensiveness, there is a "place" for self-assessment. Stand in the feelings and thoughts that naturally surface when a personal truth is uncovered and discovered. The instances when the natural reflex is to step away from the uncomfortable feelings associated with an idea or identifier are the places where authentic reflection can begin to support growth.

Recently, in conversation with someone I have known for over thirty years, I shared the idea about humans' potential for growth as a result of *standing in the discomfort* associated with an identified privilege, while personally peeling back the layers under the feeling. The person automatically replied, "But I shouldn't feel guilty about my privileges, right?" The unspoken next sentence likely included a rationale including guilty feelings potentially thwarting any personal growth on the continuum of development.

What if instead of discounting, excusing, or intellectualizing the negative feelings associated with a realized privilege, your personal commitment includes reflecting on the emotions and recognized privilege? Name the unwanted or unexpected feeling; recognize how you feel and then dig deeper, instead of masking or turning away.

Reflection requires personal curiosity, even just a bit. Seeking to understand how one personally shows up in environments, and the *why* behind those *how* truths is part of the growth journey connected with authentic reflection.

Throughout this book, you are asked to lean into presented topics with a purposeful sense of knowing and understanding your capacity for Will and Skill through a Pause and Process practice. There is not a complicated formula to apply before pausing. You are nudged to personally hold space for an internal conversation as you respond to the prompt. The intentional Pause and Process sections are placed throughout the work based on lived experiences: some shared by others, some gathered through research, and my own.

A necessary, and obvious, reminder here is our individual life experiences do not match, regardless of how closely lives were experienced. Individual backgrounds uniquely represent how each of us has encountered our world; your lived experiences are unlike anyone else's. Draw a parallel between thumbprints and lived experiences. No two individual sets are the same.

So, as you read and you come across a thought thread requiring more personal investigation, do so, even if there is not a built-in pausing place at that point in the book. When an idea or concept or data point lands in an uncomfortable or unfamiliar place for you, choose to pause and process.

Utilize the Pause and Process method to uncover, discover, and further develop your Will and Skill, and forward momentum on your continuum of personal development. Pause and Process prompts are intentionally offered to spur reflection beyond the surface level; notice the depth of personal investigation you are willing to provide, even for yourself. Notice if your reflexive response begins with thought, intellect, feeling, or belief.

Here is the first invitation, or nudge to invest in personal growth and understanding.

Pause and Process

Consider one of your life circumstances fitting under the Privileged definition. Some historical, contextual, and traditional conditions of privilege are associated with race, gender, class, sexuality, and level of education, to name just some of the possible qualifiers.

Even if you have not previously considered or owned this position of privilege, if you are aware others identify the qualifier as a point of privilege, choose to name it here:

Which position of privilege are you naming here?

1. Have you previously paused to consider how this position of privilege impacts your lived experiences? Why or why not?

   _____
   _____
   _____
   _____

2. Describe the initial feelings of naming this position of privilege.

   _____
   _____
   _____
   _____

   Part of the human experience includes emotional connections. Naming the feelings associated with an identified privilege creates opportunities to understand the emotion's point of origin or the connective tissue holding the position of privilege.

3. What conditions are necessary for you to uncover, and understand the individual privileges you hold? What is your definition of unearned privileges?

   _____
   _____
   _____
   _____

4. What are you curious about as you consider this identified privilege?

_____
_____
_____
_____

5. What resources, including other individuals, could you seek as part of the journey to understand the impact(s) of this privilege more fully?

_____
_____
_____
_____

Notice this reflective prompt does not include any connections to systems you are associated or aligned with; at this point, the reflection is intended to cause movement within you; the instinctive response might be to point outward (at managers, co-workers, policies). This reflection connection focuses on your ability to look inside, own a thought, feeling, or cluster of emotions and become curious.

Personal commitment for action is dependent on the ability to honestly ask and respond as a reflective practitioner, even when the response is uncomfortable to own . . . maybe especially when forming the question is uncomfortable.

Dominance within a community is not dictated by the number of people wielding control. Dominant culture status is upheld by systems designed to separate; those same systems have limitations around access points and opportunities for achievement. People who are minoritized are not always outnumbered; instead, minoritized people are pushed to the margins by individuals and groups with more power and status (McCarty 2005). Which creates a dominant culture way of viewing and moving through the world. For some members of the dominant culture whose lived experiences are privileged enough to have only ever stood firmly in the center, seeing the margins is not likely, and in some cases, impossible.

Ironically or serendipitously, an example of a comfortably centered position being confronted lived out for me while authoring this book. As a member of an association with a mission of creating opportunities for collaboration across multiple organizations, I served on the executive team. Multiple dimensions of diversity were represented within the organization's membership, including professional leadership roles, education, age, race, and gender.

As president of the group, I was invited into conversations with some members of the organization who are female, expressing frustrations around in-meeting comments and decisions expressed by some male members as gender microaggressions. Some of the leaders who are female[3] questioned the merit and purpose of continuing to attend the meetings while also wondering how to raise awareness within the organization.

Presuming positivity and seeking change, the executive team (of which I was the only female) agreed to add an agenda item for the upcoming meeting on equity-centered group dynamics. During the meeting, a handful of female members provided specific examples of words and instances when *othering* (real or perceived) occurred without specifically naming anyone as an offender. The only action requested by the members who brought the concern forward was more awareness around equity and inclusion from all members moving forward. Not more than ten minutes was spent on the agenda topic.

Initial, general reactions from some of the male members included cautious curiosity and apologies. I admit, I shared a concern held by some of the members brave enough to broach the topic: what would be the fallout of this brief, albeit important, discussion?

Less than a week after the meeting, I received a phone call from one of the organization members who is male. For over thirty minutes, I was on the receiving end of raised-voice accusations and complaints of allowing a "surprise attack" on the person on the other end of the phone. Reminder, not one person was specifically named or addressed during the portion of the meeting when members who are females shared their perceptions and experiences of microaggressions.

During the phone call, my leadership abilities were questioned for "allowing" the agenda item to be added, even after I explained the executive team's process and the fact protocol was followed regarding the members' request to add the equity topic. As the conversation ended, I was told to learn the difference between "unintended microaggressions and intended microaggressions" and to "never bring this topic up again."

The reflection I wrote following the phone call includes: ... *for some members of the dominant culture, standing so firmly and comfortably cushioned in the center, means it is not possible for the margins to even be seen, let alone acknowledged. He is so comfortably numb in the center he cannot see the margins and may not even fully believe margins exist.*

Another part of my reflection included owning my role in the conversation and my realization of how quickly I slid into the mode of pacifying my colleague. Understanding automatically how to navigate the conversation to maintain a supposed spirit of collaboration where none was evident.

I wrote, *How can I claim my work around creating equity-centered spaces and so adeptly slip into the role of pacifier when gender inequity is in my face? I knew how to show up in that phone call, attempting to avoid being labeled hard to work with or overly sensitive.* I minimally interrupted and weighed my responses with sounds of affirmation for his feelings. Clearly, my journey in the work is ongoing.

In her bestselling book *Caste: The Origins of Our Discontents* (2020, 388) Wilkerson reminds us, "We are responsible for our own ignorance or, with time and openhearted enlightenment, our own wisdom."

Inequitable systems are created and maintained by the people in the center. Uncentering is as much a conscious choice as is marginalizing. The counter-narrative to the previous statement is, of course, what if centering and marginalizing are not conscious choices? And within the question lies an opportunity to uncover and discover one's place on the page through self-reflection.

Individuals and groups who are minoritized are expected to uphold systemic inequity to demonstrate allegiance to the community or institution as part of their position/role/title agreements.

Within your current career field, what systems are you a part of or aware of that simultaneously elevate an opportunity for growth for some and create division among members? What systems are evaluated on standards and protocols built to maintain the centering and marginalization of people? Who is in the center in the systems you are a part of, and who decides people's placement along the continuum of inclusive or exclusive communities?

Creating communities of belonging and hope is not the work of just one person. Equity-centered belonging and bold hope are the work of each person, each of us. This community-building work begins by identifying commonly held biases, hidden just below the surface and those clearly visible for self and others. The systematic process of building personal capacity for culturally proficient work in organizations, school settings, businesses, and communities grows through personal and collective efficacy. The process acknowledges *where* each person is in relation to cultural proficiency.

Any conversation involving the education profession requires acknowledging creating inclusive communities of equity and hope-filled spaces was, for a time, considered a foundational element of the calling. The people-centered words and ideals historically considered unifying for the profession around the common good may, in this era, be leveraged against community advocates and educational leaders. Caution and concern about the oftentimes real possibility of negative ramifications may slow or prevent forward momentum and thereby encourage the status quo.

Through the learning leader lens, uncovering and discovering implicit biases is possible. Authentic opportunities for self-assessment require the courage to uncover self and institutional bias. The same evidence-based self-assessment establishes goal-building opportunities, points to next steps, and serves as calls to action along the culturally proficient leadership journey.

The goal setting process includes intentional progress monitoring protocols and personal accountability, which allows you to name, claim, and aim for personal growth. Identifying social constructs informing, and at times, driving both the progression and regression of cultural responsiveness is not a one-size-fits-all endeavor. As learning leaders accept the cultural proficiency call to create equity-centered, inclusive communities of belonging, the work begins with our individual degree of willingness to reflect.

There is no shortage of socio-political noise and negativity directed at equity, inclusion, and diversity in communities, neighborhoods, and professional spaces. The static around equity, inclusion, and diversity, and the authenticity of inclusive communities established in belonging and hope, is distracting—maybe intentionally so. Because once you name and claim your personal truths, what follows includes reconciling personal truths with individual values and actions. Who stands to gain and maintain positional status and privilege in communities when divisive static remains on high volume?

In early 2021, while facilitating a graduate studies book study utilizing three books[4] with the common elements of detangling and dismantling social injustice and white privilege, a generally quiet graduate student, a white male, suggested, "Instead of saying "privilege" why don't you use the word "opportunities"? People would like that word better. I mean, I don't have privileges, but I do have opportunities."

The graduate student in his mid-twenties, a member of the dominant culture, with at least one parent who held a prominently titled position in the community and who was himself positioned to hold a school administrator role within two years, could not *see* any privileges he held. He could not see, chose not to acknowledge, or had not yet fully developed his reflective practitioner's will and skill.

Authentic self-assessment and reflection is the space where each of us first tells ourselves the truth, or we choose not to. Authentic self-assessment and reflection are not performative and are not achieved from a distance. The heart and hard *work*, and that word is aptly applied here, is up close and personal. The reconciliation and ownership of personal truths and personally held values are not achieved through happenstance.

Rather, the deliberate processes and practices of self-reflection create opportunities for each of us to know what we are committed to doing in this world with the full light of looking inside. The inclination to remind you that reflection is meant to be real and vulnerable and sometimes messy, because people are messy. On the other hand, self-reflection is not intended to be practiced as self-torment over choices made or not made. Anguishing over choices, biases, and missteps can produce inaction and a spiral of self-incrimination. If you are stuck in the mud of previous choices, seeing a more promising path ahead is not possible. Some good news is, with intentional skill development, we learn to recognize when personal power for growth is stymied by dwelling on past missteps.

What are your non-negotiables? When faced with a complex decision or an opportunity to show up as a co-conspirator, our individual choices include the fear of ruffling feathers, personal resistance to uncovering personally held biases, and leaning into the vacuum of hopelessness, telling ourselves, "There's just nothing I can do anyway." So too, individual choices include the psyche-stabilizing alternatives of guarding the hope within and moving forward.

Chapter Takeaways

Does what you say and do each day align with your non-negotiables? If you do not check-in, self-assess in reflection, how will you know?

In knowing, you determine if there is a measurable difference between your aspirational self and your authentic self. This book is an analysis resource organized around reflective practices, equity-centered belonging, and hope, as much as it is a tool for creating spaces rooted in personal and systemic growth where individual calls to action are fuel for next steps. How will you leverage this tool toward personal growth?

Notes

1 As of March 2024, lawmakers in thirty-three states in the United States introduced and/or passed more than 100 bills regulating or restricting inclusion, equity, and diversity initiatives (nbcnews.com, 2024).
2 Emerson (1841), 52.
3 The wording structure of this sentence intentionally places the gender identity following the role of leader.
4 Including the citations for the three books generally referenced in this section adds to the validity and credibility of this book's purpose, and intentionally plants seeds for your possible next reads: Reynolds and Kendi (2020), Brown (2018), and Jensen (2005).

3 Momentum for Transformational Change

> *If not us, then who? If not now, then when?*—John Lewis

As you read the title for Chapter 3, did you feel an internal pang alerting you to some heavy cognitive lifting? No worries, this chapter does include tools and a safe place for you to engage in honest reflective practice.

Identifying systemic processes that require dismantling is the transformational work of each person striving to create communities of belonging. There are no guarantees the transformation will be easy or always create connections between the people working side by side; however, without attempts at transformation, the status quo is simply maintained. The concepts of transforming, changing, and improving are not interchangeable, especially in a thoughtful conversation about creating equity-centered communities of belonging and hope. Transformation is directly tied to reimagining and innovating. When systems, practices, and policies are improved or changed, transformation is not necessarily part of the equation. Think about a recent change touted to improve your neighborhood or organization. Likely, it is easy enough to notice the change and even understand how the change equaled improvement for some people. Transformation asks us to peel back the layers and investigate what elements are holding the current structures in place, and rather than replace those structures, reimagine and design with an innovator's mindset.

Reflection is an individual's intentional, focused thinking and writing. The process of pausing to reflect includes an individual system for moving through thought threads to create connections. Self-reflection is primarily an individually created conscious system for critical thinking. Self-reflection includes focused attention on the essence and impact of what was and/or was not done and what will or will not continue.

Self-awareness is a positive byproduct of genuine reflection nested within the ability to own personal biases. Personal accountability is a result of the systematic, introspective reflection framework offered in this book. The other side to the positive benefits of owning personal biases is the weight of the work. Owning personal biases is not a light lift. Your capacity-depth may be challenged during introspective and personal work. Throughout the reflective process, honestly naming your reality and how you arrived at your current understanding protects against confirmation bias. Personal reality checking is an element woven into the fabric of reflection. Confirmation bias is unpacked and explored in Chapter 5.

Through the investment of time, in repetition and in engaged practice, individual Will is developed. The internal driving force of Will is not externally navigated or coerced. People cannot be forced to develop a personal sense of Will or inclination to learn. The exploration of facts and diverse lived experiences framed in readiness is the key to developing Will as you take control of your thoughts and actions.

Following is another invitation or nudge for self-reflection.

Pause and Process

Think of a time you were offered an authentic glimpse inside someone's lived experience that you could not immediately relate to because the circumstance was different from any you personally encountered or even considered might exist. Maybe the opportunity to glimpse another's life experience was from a distance, such as shared on the news, at the grocery store, or in your professional setting.

Where were you when the experience was shared?
_____
_____

Who were you with?_____

1. When a lived experience is shared with you beyond your lived truth, how do you initially receive the information, as a thinker, believer, or a feeler? Do you begin personally processing the shared experience with how you feel, or with the connections and/or disconnections to your beliefs, or with the thinking part of yourself?

_____
_____
_____
_____
_____

2. Describe your willingness to openly receive someone's lived experience that is in direct contrast with systems you are/have been a part of. What are your internal processes for accepting *and* receiving another's lived truth? Note: This prompt may require acknowledging areas of personal development.

_____
_____
_____
_____
_____
_____
_____
_____

3. Describe your ability to openly receive someone's lived experience that connects with or resonates with one of your own life shaping circumstances. What are your internal processes for accepting and/or receiving another's lived truth that is close to one of your own lived experiences? What evidence do you have to qualify this description as reality, instead of aspirational?

_____
_____
_____
_____
_____
_____
_____

4. What are you curious about as the differences and similarities to your previous two responses take shape? Are there elements of your responses you are resisting? What do you notice about your responses to prompts 2 and 3 above?

_____
_____
_____
_____
_____

5. What resources, including other individuals, will you seek as part of the journey to understand the ways you connect and/or disconnect with lived experiences unlike your own? Who are your thought partners?

_____
_____
_____
_____

Authentically valuing lived experiences unlike one's own is built on believing the circumstances just as offered. Valuing another's lived experience is not conditional belief; there is not a necessity to explain the differences of the lived experience from one's own.

In McIntosh's 1989 White Privilege Survey, participants start with individual lived experiences. On the surface, lived experiences may appear similar for individuals and communities whose privileges have been offered and claimed with a sense of "of course" and "this is the way it is." Overlapping human experiences are not necessarily bound together with the sameness of privilege.

An interesting overlap of lived experiences includes both the positively and negatively framed posing of the two statements. That is, individuals at the privileged center share a common meaning to the phrases "of course" and "this is the way it is." While individuals pushed to the margins may also have a common meaning to the phrases "of course" and "this is the way it is." The polarity of definitions of the two phrases is shaped by shared lived experiences and community memberships from different perspectives on the page. The view from the center cannot be the same as that of the margins, and vice versa.

The context of one's lived experience is determined by both unearned advantages and unearned disadvantages. The extent to which an experience is fully believed by another person does not detract from the truth of the situation. If you have yet to encounter not being believed in sharing a lived experience, imagine the potential feelings of frustration, anger, and isolation woven into disbelief. While not satisfying, perhaps it is soothing to know the other person does not have to believe the experience happened for you to hold your truth.

How can equity-centered communities be built and inequitable systems dismantled when not all lived experiences are believed or carry value? The degree of belief in another's truth is an equity indicator. Read the previous sentence again and consider your initial inclination to believe someone's experience when you do not have even a distantly experienced circumstance. How long, after initial disbelief, do you stand in that space? How long after initial doubting if the experience really happened as shared, do you metaphorically sit down, listen, and begin building belief patterns?

Understanding, owning, uncovering, and/or discovering core values and non-negotiables, is the necessary first step in self-reflection. Holding the value of equity in one's core is like a beacon of light, drawing others in, just as the absence of the equity value pushes others away, casting them to the margins.

How does one identify core values and non-negotiables? Core values and non-negotiables are rooted in personal mission. Progressing on the continuum of development includes knowing and understanding what you value, need, and desire to do and be. A value is most efficiently understood as a fundamental and foundation belief, and identifying a value is the practice of defining what is important for each of us. The individually affirming non-negotiables are shown and made known through words, actions, and investments—time, emotions, thinking, resources, and the like.

The following Values Inventory exercise guides you through the self-assessment process. Complete each step without reading ahead in order to produce authentic responses.

Table 3.1 Values Inventory

Step 1. Quickly make a list of *what you truly value*, without explanation or description. Use Table 3.1, filling as many spaces as possible, use the margins to add more values, if necessary.

Values Inventory: What guides you and provides foundation for your daily decisions?

Step 2. Reread each value you identified in the Inventory. Circle the top eight; which values listed do you consider the eight most important for your individual identity? There might be a temptation to circle more than eight, resist that desire.

Table 3.2 Values Inventory Top 8

1.	2.	3.	4.
5.	6.	7.	8.

Step 3. Consider the meaning or definition each of the eight circled values holds for you. Prioritize the eight circled values in order of personal importance. Use Table 3.2 to list the eight core values in order of their greatest importance for you.

The Values Inventory exercise provides an opportunity for you to solidify, uncover, and rediscover, what closely held non-negotiables guide your daily interactions, decisions, and steps. How does knowing and owning your top eight core values align with where you are and where you are in time, place, and purpose? What do you appreciate about the Values Inventory process?

What did you notice about yourself as you completed each table? Did some non-negotiables require less thoughtful consideration to add or remove to the top eight table?

What individual life experiences drove your decision-making throughout the Values Inventory process?

A call to action is your self-determined next step... providing the opportunity to define personal priorities and focus your impact. When calls to action are externally assigned, the recipient chooses a level of investment and commitment to the outside cause. The genuine process of creating a call to action is rooted in naming and claiming one's own hope-filled, purposeful change and transformation. In his book on Gandhi's leadership lessons, Nair reminds readers of the actionable results possible with doing more than simply identifying your values, "Operationalizing values transforms them into actions" (1997, 25).

Through authentic, ongoing self-reflection, leaders of transformative change utilize Will and Skill to challenge the status quo, courageously leaning into the discomfort of uncertainty paying attention to who is and who is not at the table.

The working elements of hope-filled, purposeful, transformational change include each of the five components: Will, Skill, Vulnerability, Capacity, Courage. The mental model depicted in Figure 3.1 illustrates the momentum generated when the five personal commitments are part of your movement toward transformational change.

This mechanism of hope-filled, purposeful reimagining provides opportunities for Change Demanders. Hope lives in the spaces between darkness and inaction. When self-reflection reveals a crack, there exists an opportunity to name and claim a next step on the continuum of development. Progress is incremental and individual, fueled by hope.

Figure 3.1 Five components of hope-filled, purposeful, transformational change. Perkins (2025).

"We need hope like we need air.... But hope is not what most of us think it is. Hope is a way of thinking—a cognitive process" (Brown 2022, 97).

In the common language section of this book, a working definition of Change Demanders is provided. Change Demanders are people, individuals or groups, who assess current reality and context with a critical and open lens, using a variety of guaranteed and viable data, to bring inequity, discrimination, and exclusion into the light, and in doing so, choose not to accept the current set of circumstances ... this is the birthplace of transformation.

Only when the truth of the present circumstances, based on both qualitative and quantitative data, is revealed, acknowledged, and understood are systemic and systematic redesigns possible. Who determines which data is collected, analyzed and actionable? With what factors? What guaranteed and reliable systems of evaluations exist or are missing? In their book *Street Data*, Safir and Dugan (2021, 205) remind us, "If leading for equity is inherently emotional work, we must cultivate our capacity to sit with and honor people's feelings. Otherwise, we risk erasing their experience."

Equity as a value is rooted in the life practice of embracing and amplifying the lived experiences of others, not just those whose lived experiences resemble one's own. The conscious choice to embrace as true another's life experience requires listening to believe, not listening to contradict, rationalize, or devalue. Listen. Listen with your mind and heart open to a background, an awareness, an experience far from any you have encountered.

When a variety of people, from a variety of places, with a variety of experiences gather to share information, knowledge, and lived experiences in an equity-centered environment, invitations for participation are not necessary. Everyone understands the value of the gathering is multiplied, not divided, by the diversity of lived experiences. Likely, the metaphorical gathering place still does not guarantee access, never mind equitable partnerships. Even when a variety of people are gathered, visibility is not guaranteed, making the amplification of each individual's lived experiences impossible. When any member of a group is made to feel or deemed erased or invisible, equity is missing.

Reversing time and controlling the actions of one's ancestors is impossible; however, what *is* possible is deciding, intentionally determining, what type of ancestor we will each be. So then, we are each ancestors in training. What steps are you taking today, your future self, and those who come after you, will be grateful for, grimace at, and wonder about?

Moving forward with intentional momentum to reform and reshape current realities is a specific choice born from a place of listening and believing. If one leans into the research about group dynamics, the understanding that group behavior is a combination of individual choices creates a space for knowing and understanding role responsibility within a community.

Borrowed from the Latin word *efficācia*, efficacy is defined as "capable of fulfilling a function" according to Merriam-Webster.com (2019). Self-efficacy is the belief one has around personal abilities to achieve a goal. Collective efficacy is the belief one has about colleagues' abilities to achieve a goal together. A person's efficacious feelings and attitudes about the ability to complete tasks and responsibilities within a community are central to personal achievement and growth.

Logically, the stronger an individual's self-efficacy, the more likely the person is to persist. The relentless pursuit toward goal achievement is associated with a personality perseverance trait. Intellectually, making the leap toward a community's equity gains and level of achievement is tied to the existence of collective efficacy within the group. Collective efficacy is not possible as long as inequity exists within the group or community. In his book focusing on equity in schools, Chism (2022, 65) identifies a common thread between equity and collective efficacy, "Getting to equity won't happen unless people believe not only in themselves but also in the capability of their colleagues."

Effective and qualified leaders establish a set of standard operating procedures and routines, according to Marzano, Waters, and McNulty (2005). Respected researchers and authors on the topic of leadership have published numerous books on the subject; in fact, in 2019 Amazon.com offered over 60,000 books on leadership across all platforms. This quantifiable data indicates a public interest and curiosity in the topic and a significant amount of information available.

Yet, with the abundance of information available on how to effectively lead and the necessary components for high-quality leadership, there is a noticeable omission in resources available to identify the impact of self-assessment and reflective practices connected to cultural proficiency. Equity-centered leadership disposition is an indicator of cultural proficiency.

Chapter Takeaways

This chapter shines a spotlight on the path from improvement → to change → to transformational change. Transformational change is at the center of will and skill development, propelled forward through vulnerability, and courageous capacity building.

As you think through the efficacy lens, are you able to name your capabilities *and* the capabilities of the people you are in community with?

How will you own your role as a Change Demander by leveraging the results of your Values Inventory?

4 Unity and Human Dynamics

> *It is essential to know yourself before you decide what work you have to do.* —Stephen Covey

Do your natural talents and strengths support the story you tell and allow others to fully tell their stories? How do you know?

To focus this work intentionally on supporting possibilities around capabilities, personal growth, and learning, I constructed the Four Stages of Learning© as a coherent and systematic questioning method to discover, uncover, and recognize points on an individual learning continuum. At each of the Four Stages of Learning©, you are encouraged to fully stop at any point and create personal connections, noticing internal signals. Each of the Four Stages of Learning© is an opportunity to look in the metaphorical mirror and self-reflect.

By this point in the reading, you may have encountered more than one idea or concept representing a speed bump in your thoughts or feelings or beliefs based on your life experiences. The so-called internal speed bumps are signals around the potential and ongoing development of critical personal and social consciousness. Engage in the Four Stages of Learning© related to the reading and your contextual understanding up to this point.

The Four Stages of Learning©

Check in with yourself in relation to ideas and concepts you have encountered in this reading:

What are you learning about yourself?

_____

_____

_____

_____

What are you *re*learning about yourself?

_____
_____
_____
_____

What are you *un*learning about yourself?

_____
_____
_____
_____

What are you *resisting* learning about yourself?

_____
_____
_____
_____

Holding ourselves able and capable to engage in self-reflection begins with an authentic examination of personally held resistance points. The vulnerability of naming a personal point of resistance is not admitting to a failure or an indication of misplaced values. What if each time you recognize or realize a resistance touchpoint, you claim the point as a place for future learning? A truth about unconscious and implicit bias is a person might live years in a false narrative built and fed on bias before the light cast by self-reflection exposes the truth.

The Four Stages of Learning© are ordered in a deliberate and measured system aimed at personal growth and understanding. The first authentic investment in asking and answering the four questions identifying the Stages of Learning might feel more cognitively labor-intensive than expected or, conversely, seem easy and not at all daunting. Even this, the measuring of how you "show up" the first few times to respond to the Four Stages of Learning©, might serve as a thought thread for future reflections.

Leaning into the fourth question of the Four Stages of Learning© includes the ability and capability to name the root of any resistance you have been holding onto without an acute awareness. Resistance ≠ failure. Are ideas, emotions, actions, reactions, or ownership causing resistance? Notice when resistance is masked behind oversimplification or, the opposite, intellectualization. Create and hold space for recognizing inequitable practices, states of being, and systems. Notice when individual defensiveness dominates and builds barriers to your learning.

The definition Marzano, Waters, and McNulty (2005) provide for a purposeful community includes a group of people with established routines, who share collective efficacy while maximizing resources. Based on the definition for a purposeful community, are you able to make personal connections with the organizations you are a part of?

In 2024, Merriam-Webster's online dictionary definition of community included thirteen subcategories. Definitions of community include coming together with common goals, joining in unity, and establishing or holding mutual goals. Throughout history, communities have formed out of necessity, and not always for goodwill. Throughout human existence, some communities were founded and constructed under false parameters, and forced upon people. Some communities are born of privilege, and some communities are established to exert dominance over another group or set of people.

The positively framed definition of community within this book is a group of people with intersecting humanity-based characteristics, linked by self and/or others. The research fueling this is the essence of belonging in communities with authentic connections rooted in the shared value of equity for each member.

Listed in Maslow's (1943, 1968) hierarchy of needs shown in Figure 4.1, belonging is a human need rooted in connection and according to the research, it must be present before esteem and self-actualization are possible. In his earlier work, Maslow introduced the concept of human hierarchical needs without the pyramid image widely used to depict his theory. As humans, we "will hunger for affectionate relations with people in general,

Figure 4.1 Five levels of needs. Maslow (1943).

namely, for a place in his group, and he will strive with great intensity to achieve this goal" (Maslow 1943, 381).

For decades psychologists and social scientists studied human and organizational tendencies around definable categories of communities and, at times, included humanity's propensity for belonging. Baumeister and Leary (1995, 497)[1] research on belonging cemented existing literature to the empirical data of their study with clear findings highlighting the "pervasive drive" humans carry to form meaningful, interpersonal relationships.

Belonging research includes understanding individuals not only seek experiences with ongoing, positive, meaningful personal impact, but they also often have an innate ability to notice when the sense of belonging is missing. Credible and sustaining belonging frameworks honor individuals' needs around the context of human dynamics. While belonging research clearly identifies the connective tissue of each individual's thoughts, feelings, and actions with the motivation to belong, there is not a *single* recipe for achieving a stable place of belonging.

Belongingness, as a fundamental human need, is not singularly achieved. This is an *all hands on deck* mindset when each member's essentialness is not diminished to cast others in a more favorable position. Yet, without intentionally examining processes and policies through an equity-valued lens, everyday systems go against people's core desire to belong, simultaneously creating silos of separation.

Cultural and individual differences require community builders to first seek to know and honor individuals. Anytime the goal of joining individuals together in community includes the essential quality of belonging, authentic relationships form around mission, vision, and common goals. Intentionally creating community is not happenstance. When we build a community, everyone's life experiences not only matter; the individual experiences become the glue holding the group together.

Think of one "place" you know you *belong*. When you think of that place, recognize the feelings evoked. Moving into your thinking self, how do you "know" you belong in that place? When you can capture the feelings and thoughts you have as you reflect on the place(s) you are confident you belong, you have the ability to create the momentum of belonging and share it with others.

Just as you are able to identify *where* you belong, you are just as able to identify instances, places, or with specific people when you did not belong (Figure 4.2). Belonging happens when we are in spaces where equity and hope serve as anchors to community building. Belonging thrives where the values of equity and hope are in the connective tissues of the group.

The opposite is also true; when the necessary components for belonging are missing, an equity-centered community cannot be established. Without belonging, human nature prompts us to do all that is possible to ensure personal safety and security. When belonging is missing, individuals within the group, organization, or system are not seen, known, or valued. *Belonging uncertainty* (Walton and Cohen, 2007) undermines individuals' goals and interrupts potential growth and group cohesion.

In their work on belonging and dignity, Cobb and Krownapple (2019) refer to the void created when authentic belonging is missing as the belonging gap. The power and potential unlocked when we are able to move up and through the personal growth model, reaching esteem and self-actualization, are not possible when belonging is missing. The elements of belonging, when authentic, are bridge builders for individual and community advancement.

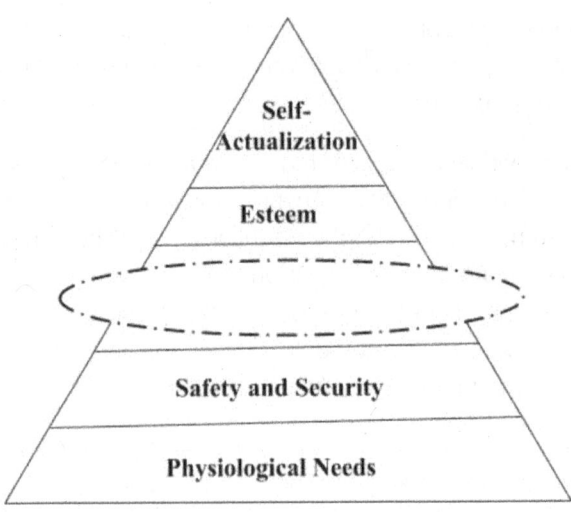

Figure 4.2 Absence of belonging. Adapted Maslow (1943).

"Cultivate belonging and we will create inclusion. Create inclusion and we will have the foundation to achieve equity" (Cobb and Krownapple 2019, 202).

The universal range of belonging and hope includes slightly tentative first steps, subject to daily ups and downs, as you navigate the terrain of everyday unpredictability. However, as confidence in hope-filled understanding increases, and your grip on the power of hope becomes more assured, the context of hope-filled belonging causes steady dependability.

What are you doing to be a part of building a hope-filled context and equity-centered community where you are now? What is your personal thumbprint on the environments people long to be a part of? Not just people who look like you or match your social identities. Dismantling inequitable systems starts with the momentum created by the diverse thoughts, attitudes, and feelings associated with belonging and hope.

Disrupting inequity begins by holding the value of hope.

Self-reflection is a mirror. Each of us decides how closely we are willing to examine our thoughts, feelings, beliefs, and actions. The power of personally held beliefs cannot be overlooked. Our individual beliefs affect what selects and determines our starting point in problem-solving and idea development. We each act based on individual beliefs, whether we take the time to intentionally reflect and identify our personally held beliefs. Establishing Belief statements is a frequent practice in the continuous improvement movement. A model for a Belief statement is:

I believe (in) _____; therefore, I _____.

Ex. I believe in culturally proficient leadership; therefore, I actively seek to identify and deconstruct inequitable systems.

Ex. I believe self-reflection is a way maker; therefore, I pause and process regularly and consistently (even when it feels uncomfortable).

Are you able to name your beliefs and align those beliefs with actions? Has the company, organization, or school setting you are a part of identified core beliefs and named what those beliefs look like in action? If you have not recently taken the time to clearly name your beliefs and how you live those beliefs, consider this your invitation to create your top three to five Belief statements.

"It is easy to believe in something intellectually, but living your beliefs takes a commitment" (Nair 1997, 27). Purpose and beliefs are fundamental pieces of self-reflection and must be focused on impact. Individual equity-centered impact is developed and strengthened through authentic self-reflection.

Locate your tools with intentional reflection to meet people where they are, not necessarily where it would be most comfortable for you. The two values of equity and hope are the foundational roots of equity-centered communities. Belonging happens in spaces where equity and hope are valued. Who are you in community with, and what values are known and held, internally and collectively?

What signals, overt or subtle, are existing community members sending to potential or actual new members? Who is signal-checking? What monitoring and evaluation systems are in place to not only member-check but also protocol-check through an equity-centered lens? As leaders develop processes and policies with an intentional nod toward inclusivity and equity-centered communities of belonging, whose primary responsibility is guaranteeing virtue signaling is not the actual status quo? How are role responsibilities designed and delegated to ensure the words written into processes and systems are more than just performance?

Positive psychology theory (Seligman 2011) is the scientific study of strengths and desired characteristics that contribute to thriving individuals and communities. The well-being theory attached to positive psychology theory reported by Seligman (2011) adds to this book's conceptual framework by supplying part of the working definition of a thriving community. The five factors attached to well-being: positive emotions, engagement, relationships, meaning and purpose, and accomplishment are intentionally associated with personal satisfaction and a sense of belonging in this research.

Lawler (1994) found satisfaction to include drive theory components and need theories. The framework of this book moves away from the idea that a perfect 50/50 balance of personal and professional responsibilities and input/output equals satisfaction. Rather, the working definition offered here for satisfaction includes the sense of fulfillment that occurs through self and collective efficacy, attitude, well-being, achievements, and recognitions.

Determination of satisfaction areas with the investment of time, expertise, care, and commitment have a greater impact on one's overall well-being than the unlikely quest for a perfect balance. There are times in life when one area or aspect requires more attention and intention than another area, that is part of the lived experience. So, rather than wear the heavy baggage of self-recrimination because one area took time from another, define, and decide how you want to spend your time. How we spend our time equals our purpose. Hope-filled purpose connects to personal satisfaction in relationship to time investments.

Authentic communities do not exist without the shared value of equity. The internal desire to enhance life experiences includes how people join in community. For some people, the internal desire is fueled by a sense of belonging and maybe more accurately *the need* to belong (Allen et al. 2022). The need to belong and matter within a chosen group is woven together with each of our individual identities. Consider the connections humans make to and with each other in thriving communities of well-being. The capacity to create thriving communities begins, and sometimes ends, with each person's will to develop the necessary skills to maintain membership within the community. Reaching back to research spanning more than thirty years (Baumeister and Leary 1995) points to the compelling human needs for belonging; many human actions are intricately linked to the need to authentically belong.

The systemic processes associated with creating opportunities for human connection and belonging include official policies and unofficial practices. How do equity-centered policies and protocols get measured for implementation success? In studying the lasting impacts of *Brown v. Board of Education* (1954) demonstrated on college campuses, a 2014 study found cross racial interactions increased the sense of belonging for students of color and white students. "... a core element of our quality of life" (Strayhorn and Johnson 2014). What does this core of belonging look like, sound like and feel like for people and groups who have been historically and are in present-day minoritized?

Who is signal-checking and who is gatekeeping? Gatekeepers are those within the community, organization, or setting who control access. In the organizational, business, or educational setting you relate to, is there an understanding that each role includes the responsibility for creating inclusive and equity-centered communities of belonging? While the responsibility to create and maintain equity-centered environments rests with all members of the community, organization or educational setting, each individual decides the extent of her active participation in the community building systems.

Adjusting the equity, diversity, and inclusion framework to include belonging as an element of the equity focus within an organization is a growing phenomenon in the United States. In 2024, US corporations reframing diversity, equity, inclusion efforts to include belonging created a fast-growing market for Employee Resource Groups (ERGs). A top-performing ERG tasked with managing social corporate responsibilities in the United States reports 86 percent of leaders in North American corporations consider fostering community and belonging as critical in social awareness extensions of businesses and agencies.[2] Are you experiencing a reimagined diversity, equity, inclusion and belonging framework in your professional setting?

In stark contrast to the business sector data representing an increase in Corporate America's focus on inclusion and belonging, a US governmental decision in March 2024 included the US House of Representatives' Office of Diversity and Inclusion formal disbandment. The decision to dissolve the office was tied to a government spending bill. Moreover, the dissolution of the Office of Diversity and Inclusion is indicative of the politicization of efforts and initiatives centered on the value of equity.

In a statement issued by the US Joint Center for Political and Economic Studies the undermining of inclusion and diversity work explicitly stated disappointment at the ODI closing,

> *Following the passage of the government spending bill, this disbandment deals a significant blow to the U.S. House Office of Diversity and Inclusion's bipartisan efforts since 2020 in promoting diverse hiring within the U.S. House offices. This decision jeopardizes the establishment of policies to support diverse communities and threatens the pursuit of inclusivity for all Americans. The dissolution of the ODI is not just a bureaucratic decision but a stark symbol of a regressive agenda undermining our call for more diversity and inclusiveness in congressional offices.*[3]

Community and family engagement is part of equity work in spaces where people in positional power roles honor equity as a value. The clear signals sent by leadership to indicate levels of investment in creating an equity-centered, anti-racist, multicultural institution are standards built into the mission and vision of the organization. The performative aspect of simply *using* the words moves to actionable when multiple measures for effectiveness are part of the systematic process. Members of an equity-centered community share a common point, rooted in being individually seen and knowing they belong, framed by multiple dimensions of diversity.

When differences are seen as assets, not deficits, there is no need to try to fit in for acceptance.

The element of time may be used as a convenient excuse for some individuals who are comfortable with the rate or lack of forward progress. If we wait for the people who own positional power to move the system, we passively accept the system as-is. However, the influence of changemakers is not evenly distributed, and the burdens caused by the inequitable systems are not evenly distributed.

In the book *We Want to Do More Than Survive: Abolitionist Teaching and the Pursuit of Educational Freedom* (Love 2019), a metaphor highlighting the automatic replenishing of privileges depicts the unevenness of the human experiences. "White privilege is like an invisible, weightless knapsack of special provisions, maps, passports, codebooks, visas, clothes, tools, and blank checks" (Love 2019, 95).

In late 2023, during one of my national presentations on the topic of this book, a participant reminded everyone in the room, "As a Muslim woman of color, I do not always have the ability to voice my concerns about the system I am a part of. My job could be at stake." She was, in part, providing a call to action for the people in the room who would not face similar consequences based on unearned privileges associated with race. The feeling of ethical tension exists in the space between knowing what the next right step is and taking the next right step.

Creating an equity-centered community is not always as simple as isolating race or gender or accessibility needs or any of the other qualifications used to describe and categorize people. What are the primary metrics you use to name the multiple layers of your identity? What are the primary metrics you use for others in your work, social circles for identifying others?

Privilege is a potential space maker in any given social circle or environment. Look around; what is your area of privilege? Realizing and recognizing spaces of held privilege as a space maker is a pathway to widening the lanes of accessibility and welcome. Actively engage in contemplative practice of prioritizing self-reflection. How do you or will you live in a way that challenges systemic privileges? How will you bring others with you?

The "I'm colorblind" response for some members of the dominant culture is like the default autocorrect response on an electronic device. Unless one is truly unable to visually see, the inability to physically see someone's skin color does not exist. Instead, people who claim to be "colorblind" do possess the reflexive response of "seeing" skin color, quickly followed by an internal reminder to pretend not to see skin color or say they do not see skin color for whatever personally held reason. While a dominant culture rationale for the colorblind trope is offered as an attempt to equalize the rationale, in fact, becomes an erasure. One cannot be colorblind and anti-racist.

At the outset of this book, I made a commitment to share pieces of my story, meeting you in the moment, even when the personal experiences are underdeveloped times in my life when I missed the goal entirely. The "colorblind" topic represents an authentic example of a time when I was certainly living in the resistant to learning stage of the Four Stages of Learning©. Earning my undergraduate degree in secondary education in 1990, brimming with the prose and poetry of writers like James Baldwin, T. S.

Eliot, Langston Hughes, and Sylvia Plath, I felt confident walking into my first interview as a prospective English and language arts teacher.

The first-time nervousness I felt interviewing for a position in the same public school district I attended as a student was mostly calmed by my self-confidence; I knew in my bones I was "ready" for *my own classroom*. The smiling middle school principal who greeted me with an outstretched hand at his office door was a man of color in his late thirties. Having already cleared the human resources interview portion of the hiring process, I remember thinking this conversation with the principal would be far more relaxed, and it probably was intended to be so. What I did not realize at the time, one of my personally held unconscious biases would be pouring out as ungracefully as spilling coffee down the front of my shirt.

"How do you create a classroom atmosphere welcoming students of multiple races?" he asked, hands folded, leaning forward on his desk. Without hesitating, I replied with an overly proud smile, "I don't see color. I treat all my students the same." The early in her career, blue-eyed, white female I was felt so good about my response. *So good*. Until he repeated part of my response back to me as a question, "You don't see color?"

I vividly remember thinking the principal asked me to expand my answer because he could not believe I was "that good" as a young professional. I imagined the principal thinking my "developed" stance represented a seasoned teacher's response, not someone at the beginning of her career. The rest of the interview passed without impact on my memory. As I drove away, the exchange between the middle school principal and myself about "not seeing color" lingered with me.

Needless to say, I was not offered that teaching position. I accepted another middle school teaching position in the same public school district. The seventh-grade English and Language Arts classroom I served in with students whose abilities to collaborate and create connections with one another taught me a great deal about belonging and community; honestly, more than I taught them about the literary devices woven throughout *The Call of the Wild* (London 1903).

I witnessed firsthand from a few hundred students in seventh grade how people with diverse racial, ethnic, and socio-economic identities could, and did, recognize differences among people exist. Creating new possibilities for human connection happens when we fully *see* one another and honor differences as opportunities to learn from, with, and about each other.

Over three decades later, I am *painfully aware* of the depths of my white privilege during the job interview for my first teaching position. I inwardly apologize and outwardly cringe thinking of the systematic whiteness I blindly and blatantly owned when I unwittingly exposed a layer of personal bias. I confidently looked a man of color, with positional authority and significantly more professional expertise, in the eyes and told him I did not see color.

I was wrong. The scope of grace I was offered that day is not lost on me. I clearly had much more growing, reflecting, and learning ahead of me.

The actions associated with anti-racist efforts cannot exist without first seeing color differences. In other words, it is not possible to be anti-racist and pledge not to see skin color. Seeing skin color differences is only a negative if by doing so reflexively it causes you to think and behave negatively toward another person based on the color of her skin. The dimensions of diversity among people only divide when humans equate "different than self" as *less than* or *wrong*.

The link between self-serving interests and racial power dates back to 1606, when the word (and social construct) of Race was formally defined in a European dictionary.[4] Race is a power construct. Racial power structures, like the other *-isms* and identity-based phobias, create and support ungrounded hierarchies and othering.[5] Throughout this writing there is a repeated call to action of seeking, believing, and amplifying others' life experiences and backgrounds. More specifically, the call includes seeking a variety of life experiences, believing the experiences shared with you, and amplifying the voices of those willing to share their story. The next layer of understanding and application of this call to action is tied to inquiry, empathy, and legitimacy. "While perspective taking is not easy, it can be accomplished.... It also requires believing that what we see is *one* view of the world, not *the* view" (Brown 2007).

Who are you in the community with? Who are you not in community with? What environmental factors influenced and continue to influence how you show up in the world? I am not suggesting a Pollyanna viewpoint or perspective implying if the red carpet is rolled out wide enough to make metaphorical room for everyone, instant community forming will occur. Frankly, unrealistic expectations or oversimplification devalues the energy and impact of authentic self-reflection. This work is not to deny hate exists. Moreover, this is not a denial of the inequity of benefits some systems provide and the comfortably numb place in the center for those benefactors. This work is a call to action around self-reflection and owning your membership within any group or community of which you are a part. If we do not individually pause, look inside *and* outside, how do we know where we stand?

Chapter Takeaways

Defining specific calls to action around seeking, believing, and amplifying others' life experiences and backgrounds moves ideas and "maybe someday" thinking toward the zone of measurable outcomes.

Moving past performance to action starts with your first step forward. Have you experienced ethical tension between engagement in active equity-centered community building and passively supporting the status quo? What does empathetic inquiry include for you?

Notes

1 Baumeister's and Leary's (1995) research "The need to belong: Desire for interpersonal attachments as a fundamental human motivation" is considered a turning point in belonging studies for the groundbreaking results identifying humanity's universal need to belong; the duo's research profoundly changed understanding around the need to belong and the direct link to thinking, feeling, and behavior patterns.

2 Source: Benevity.com is the leading US ERG, a resource for insights into corporate purpose and social impact trends and reporting the increase in corporate awareness around fostering community and belonging.

3 https://jointcenter.org/joint-center-responds-to-the-u-s-house-office-of-diversity-and-inclusion-disbandment/

4 "Race . . . means descent. Therefore, it is said that a man, a horse, a dog, or another animal is from a good or bad race." Jean Nicot, *Trésor de la langue française*, 1606.

5 "Othering is a term that not only encompasses the many expressions of prejudice on the basis of group identity . . . it provides a clarifying frame that reveals a set of common processes and conditions that propagate group-based inequality and marginality." Powell and Menendian (2016).

5 What Is Missing and What Is Needed?

How does what you say and do each day align with your non-negotiables? Creating a case for self-reflection through the active connection to the Four Stages of Learning© is the *inside work* mentioned throughout this reading. In the middle of an uncomfortable and needed conversation, it is necessary to pause and assess which stage of learning is being experienced. What might you be pretending not to see or know?

Inclusivity and equity-centered communities of hope and belonging are goals only attained through intentional first steps, then next steps, and next steps. Where are you welcome to speak your truth and experiences? Where is speaking your truth and lived experiences ill-advised or entirely not possible? How do you navigate in environments where you are admitted and not welcome. It is not possible to listen and learn from others' lived experiences when divisiveness is the go-to mechanism.

Scattered pockets of community and hourglass-shaped communities are the opposite of equity-centered spaces and places. The gaps between clusters of community are reduced and removed with a shared focus and determination of individuals who value equity and bold hope. Welcoming others whose viewpoints, experiences, and perspectives differ from your own creates and sustains equity-centered communities. Push past the fear of *getting it wrong* and start the conversation. When we choose to lean out of our comfort zone, no longer passively accepting divisive tactics baked into long-standing systems, we claim unity for humanity.

In Part II, the data serving as a foundation for this book, directly related to belonging and hope, is shared, identifying the connecting elements of personal investment in fully seeing others and being seen. The hundreds of personal data points collected for this work clearly point to the connection we each seek. We want to see and be seen. We want to know and be known. And, as evidenced in the data for this and other research on belonging and hope, connection—connection with one another—is the link each of us seek.

> *Very few of us want to continue down the path of separation, or to contribute to more hatred and aggression. If we're going to reweave the world rather than have it disintegrate, we need new ways to understand diversity and differentness. What if we approached each other from our uniqueness? (Wheatley 2002, 105)*

What do you need to know and what do you need to do in spaces where multiple perspectives are offered, believed, and valued? When a community is facing a tough time, who shows up? And why do others not show up?

Lean into the following invitation to Pause and Process around the possibility of ethical tension. Notice the connections you clearly make and the connections you feel inclined to avoid.

Pause and Process

Recall a professional circumstance you were a part of when an individual or group was not granted access to resources or possibilities within the community because of the actions (or lack of) by someone with role authority.

Where were you? _____

How long had you been a member of the community/organization?
_____

1. What formal and informal practices and/or protocols were leveraged for limiting access?

   _____
   _____
   _____
   _____

2. What practices and/or protocols could have been leveraged to create a sense of belonging within the community for the denied individual or group?

   _____
   _____
   _____
   _____

3. What were the intended outcomes of the limited or denied access? What were the actual outcomes of the limited or denied access?

_____
_____
_____
_____

4. What are you curious about as you consider access in this situation?

_____
_____
_____
_____

5. What resources, including other individuals, will you seek as part of the journey to understand points of access more fully?

_____
_____
_____
_____

As individuals within a community begin honing reflective practices, the sense of awareness for self, systems, and others naturally increases. The ability to name and own individual role responsibilities for creating communities for belonging and hope are expanded through the effective steps of understanding personal backgrounds and how we each experience life . . . creating connections. Does increasing awareness of role responsibilities within a community begin to shape community cohesiveness? When individuals within the community understand the human dynamics within the group, who leverages positional authority with an equity-centered lens, rooted in measurable actions?

Identifying which systems permit limited access for individuals outside the community and how those systems are maintained are calls to action for Change Demanders. How is access defined in your setting? What systemic processes remain in place that are predictable in patterns of limited or denied access? "Do we teach and lead to simply reproduce reality, or will we teach and lead to transform it" (Safir and Dugan 2021, 4)?

The continuum of development is like the speedometer of a vehicle. In this instance, the continuum of development indicates increasing levels of knowledge. The continuum of development is a combination of one's lived experiences, curiosity, reflection, the Will and Skill capacity to learn more, understand and believe others' lived experiences, and amplify lived experiences that are other than one's own.

The intersection of humanity occurs at the point where what you value, and I value, and she values, and they value, matters to each of us enough that we intentionally and naturally come together in spaces where each voice is amplified to the same volume.

In the amplification of each lived experience, seeds for communities of belonging are planted. Checking in with self through reflection, in an ongoing and systematic process, creates opportunities for communities of belonging and hope to grow. Group behavior is really a collection of individual choices, influenced by those we routinely and predictably spend time with, personally and professionally.

The historical stumbling blocks preventing valuing another's lived experience as much as one's own are based on fear, power, privilege, unearned advantages, and unearned disadvantages. Power is a positive fuel for moving forward and creating change, unless the power is wielded over a group or groups of people for the benefit of the dominant group. Ideas and ideals in the name of change cause opposition and resistance by status quo defenders.

Equity cannot be gained without power. Power exists in social status, social acceptance, social structures, and equal access. Power exists within each person; sometimes role authority grants more power of responsibility; however, the same role responsibility that could positionally remove equity holds the potential to add access.

There is power in connections. Notice the missing qualifiers from the previous statement. There is power in negative connections and there is power in positive connections. This is an example of both dichotomies being true. Personally assess which power lane fuels your momentum. Where is your attention, with what intention, and with what level of investment for a particular desired outcome?

When one person or group holds dominance over another, not only is each lived experience not lifted, the value of lived experience is lost in the shuffle. The coexistence of unity and humanity are lost when individuals lack will, skill, and capacity to hold oneself able to deepen individual knowledge banks of understanding.

How do individuals make space for personal growth through reflection, for personal accountability through skill and capacity development, for creating systems of personal change? The heart and hard work of skill development and expanding capacity is cultivated through authentic reflection. Believing in the possibility of changing another's will and ability solely through accountability measures is counterfactual. Look no farther than the research connecting instruction and assessment.

The measure for determining effective instruction is guaranteed assessment, and the inverse is also true. The teaching, learning and assessment practices that happen in isolation are ineffectual. Compare that process of development and understanding to the principles associated with community building, for intentionally built systems of equity and inclusion.

"Our companies, our relationships, and our lives are mirrors accurately reflecting us back to ourselves" (Scott 2017, 95).

How do individuals and communities know when space is equally distributed in such a way that people of goodwill and positive intention are able to create communities of belonging and hope? Self-reflection includes understanding one's place in the world, the arrival point, what privileges, opportunities, and advantages (earned and unearned) you are a product of or are currently benefiting from. At each step in self-reflection, a personal challenge to interrogate reality is crucial. Check in with self to gauge awareness of truth or aspirational thinking. Reflection is not about perfection; in fact, just the opposite is true. Self-reflection is always about progress and not about perfection. Focus on progress. Aspiring for perfection is a roadblock and a barrier to even identifying growth points along the way. Not everything will go according to plan. And when your solid plan fails, how do you hold on to the hope of trying again? In his 1968 address in Washington, DC, Rev. Dr. King said, "We must accept finite disappointment, but never lose infinite hope."

> **Potential prompt for your next self-reflection: Progress
>   Perfection**
> - How do you monitor your progress, and what criteria do you use as measurement tools?
> - What is the scope of your grace, for yourself and the people in your community?
> - How do you demonstrate grace when confronted with imperfections?

The next leverage point in the mechanism of creating communities of belonging and hope occurs when the reflective practitioner looks around, and truly sees and understands who is standing with her. Who is not standing with her, who decided and who continues to make the decision?

Focus determines direction. Impact is measured by an individual's attention, intention, and language skills. The truth about focus is enveloped in the tendency of human nature to either seek that which affirms and confirms personal beliefs and lived experiences, or in the curiosity to discover new viewpoints and opportunities for knowledge building. The impact barometer is established through intentional critical thinking and thoughtful thinking. Thinking outside the limiting boxes of current understanding and thoughtfully considering inclusive systems designed and built to include all members of the community, not just the historically centered members.

Regardless of position, each of us is called to recognize equity-centered, efficacious conditions through the solution-focused lens. Conversations about intent and impact are not new. Prioritizing the people in the center with intent and impact considerations means the individuals and groups held to the margins are not systematically considered or are not considered from a place of authentic knowing. The very nature of belonging, conveying intentional membership within a community, is vested in seeking, seeing, believing, and amplifying the lived experiences of all members.

Effective communication and collaboration are foundational elements in the continuum of development for creating communities of belonging and hope. The measurement of language skill on the continuum of development allows individuals to assess personal and systemic bias, focus, and growth. Systems for intentional reflection is a personal communication method with oneself.

What are you aiming for? While not every attempt lands center on the target, no one aims for the edges of the bull's eye. Reflection is not about accepting and celebrating the status quo. Rather, reflection is about pausing to process where you are on your personal continuum of growth and understanding. Determining and discerning personal location in relationship to goal attainment, necessary next steps, measuring and evaluating growth happens when we lean into the courageous act of self-reflection.

If we are not willing to invest in understanding where we individually stand on the continuum of development, how does anyone really know which direction they are headed on the pathway to creating communities of belonging and hope, or if that is even the path you are currently traveling?

When was the last time you were curious? Really curious. Inquisitive interest, otherwise referred to as curiosity, might be used as your personal learning barometer. People are inherently curious about what they want to know more about. When a person is no longer genuinely curious about a topic, new knowledge is no longer sought, and if gained, that knowledge quickly gets mentally sorted into the *I am skeptical* filing cabinet drawer of our mind and most often disregarded as an uncertain truth.

Seeking new knowledge from a different vantage point does not have to lead to confirmation bias. We personally reap the benefits of confirmation bias when the information we seek merely confirms what we already know or suspect on the topic. We get more of what we look for in most circumstances, so seeking new knowledge requires looking outside the spotlight we personally shine on the topic.

A fixed mindset (Dweck 2008, 7) is limiting and impedes initiatives for progress, reform, or change. "Although people may differ . . . in initial talents, aptitudes, interests or temperaments, everyone can change and grow through application and experience." Curiosity levels point to possible areas of growth. What are you curious about? What are others on the team and in the organization curious about? How do you know?

Of course, a book built on the value of equity must be transparent enough to name the privilege associated with the idea of areas of growth. Consider a comment made during a discussion on systemic bias by a graduate student studying educational leadership. "We all have the opportunity to make our lives whatever we want," the student offered by way of emphasizing the potential of unlimited mindsets, while unknowingly *resisting* the discussion topic of dominant culture structures centering some people and intentionally marginalizing others.

Presuming positivity, I want to believe the graduate student's contribution originated from a place of believing in the intrinsic promise and possibility within each of us. This type of thinking, however misguided, unintentionally perpetuates and rejects the evidence around systemic "othering" and limited achievement options for people who are marginalized and minoritized. "Remember that lowering standards doesn't raise students' self-esteem. But neither does raising standards without giving students ways of reaching them" (Dweck 2008, 212).

That which gets measured, gets accomplished. When a goal is identified without the next steps and progress monitoring processes clearly established, the results, if named, are guesses at best, and arbitrary accidents at worst. There are success criteria toward skill building as a reflective practitioner. Creating a personal system for reflection is measured in the structure of the reflection, as well as designing a reflective process with topic identification and topic connections with personal values and goals.

Intentional self-reflection based on will, skill, knowledge, and language capacity requires a systematic, consistent process. Reflective practice is like flexing a thought building muscle. The routines established around how and when one pauses to reflect over time become systems geared toward personal and professional growth and development. The research around reflection dates as far back as 1933 when John Dewey wrote, "We do not learn from experience; we learn from reflecting on experience."

By choosing to pause and process, individuals are creating spaces to monitor and adjust decision-making and value adding potentials to and within the community.

Figure 5.1 includes a mental model for self-exploration, supporting reflective practitioners movement through intentional practice. Mental models are often created and leveraged by people when an idea or concept is introduced or discovered at a deeper than previously understood level. The Reflective Process offered in this writing is a systematic guide. The intentional act of bridging thoughts and experiences with feelings, values, attitudes, and perceptions is at the heart of self-reflection.

Figure 5.1 The Reflective Process. Perkins (2025).

Self-reflection is not journaling. The intentional and personal skill-builder of self-reflection is a stopping place for connecting ideas, beliefs, and thoughts with the layers of learning. Questioning self and systems is woven into the fabric of this skill-building practice. The systematic process of self-reflection is punctuated by naming the next steps, with specificity, so your practices intentionally shift. Identifying your next step matters, even when the first next step is the only one known.

The Reflective Process wheel (Figure 5.1) supports the prompts and thought threads for your potentially deeper development nested within each section.

1. Name!

    Identify a circumstance from your current reality, personal or professional. This experience could be a new or recurring thought, a recent conversation, an observation you make in your setting, a meeting, an email, a phone call, or a recent decision- made by you, or for you; thereby, impacting you. This portion of the reflection is simply a brief description and may be accomplished in a few sentences.

2. Connect!

   In this section individuals analyze the circumstance(s), noticing connections through reflection. Consider the situation or conditions identified in the first section; what are the existing links to your current understanding, beliefs, values, intentions? How does this new connection or set of connections create opportunities for individual deeper understanding? What might be the implications if no further action is taken? What are the growth implications for self and others? Why does this circumstance matter?

3. Learn!

   Section three of the Reflective Process utilizes the four phases of learning constructed in my work, and requires the reflective practitioner to focus on self in relation to the topic: What am I learning? Unlearning? Relearning? Resisting learning? Each of the four levels of learning should be identified in this section of the written reflection as the practitioner takes ownership of personal learning.

   This section of the reflective process specifically focuses on taking ownership of personal learning. That is, in this section of the reflection, asking and answering all four learning layers questions is requisite to moving forward as a reflective practitioner.

4. Do!

   This is the action phase of the reflective cycle. Practitioners are called to name next steps with specificity of time, people, and resources, along with systems for monitoring and evaluating progress. Without specificity, this section of the reflective process is passive and aspiration, not actionable. How will the named next step(s) support personal efforts and create momentum toward communities of belonging and hope?

The last section of self-reflection moves farther than owning the learning, toward leveraging the possibilities of growth and change. How will your individual actions change because of this intentional connection and learning? How will you know? What are the logical next steps? What are the courageous next steps? What are the uncomfortable next steps? What does personal accountability look like, sound like, and feel like? How will you hold yourself able, capable, and accountable?

The four-pronged Reflective process repeats as part of an ongoing personal practice to check in with self, monitor understanding, and recognize belief connections/disconnects with systems and circumstances. Each section of the reflective process is intended to build on itself, with each portion more fully developed than the previous.

Initially, naming the circumstance might seem easier to describe; logically, knowing something is not landing well inside is less internally challenging than owning "why" the unsettled response occurs. The Name! section is shorter in length than sections Connect! Learn! and Do! As the momentum created throughout the process creates opportunities for more in-depth discovery about self, circumstances, and systems.

The first time I was required to systematically and consistently practice self-reflection occurred during the early studies of my master's degree work. The requirement to write a reflection for twenty-one consecutive days seemed daunting. I wondered how I might "hoop jump" this part of the course . . . and then I started writing the first reflection. Supplied with a prompt around being a graduate student which, for me, simultaneously also included the professional roles of full-time middle school teacher, Language Arts department chair, yearbook sponsor, and team leader; I also owned the roles of wife and mom with four kids ranging in ages from six years to sixteen years.

As a fledgling graduate student, the systematic, reflective process allowed (honestly, maybe "forced" is a more apt word choice) me to initially uncover the fear of failing at any portion of graduate school and maintaining the rest of my life responsibilities. The fear of letting my family down or not holding up my professional responsibilities filled the "so what" portion of my first few reflections.

I will not gloss over the learning layers I needed to unpack during those first weeks of required self-reflection. I tackled the raw thoughts and feelings of imposter syndrome, mom guilt, and female leadership uncertainty, to name a few, and discovered the more I leaned into the practice of reflection, the more I was able to see possibilities and opportunities for ownership, growth, and action on my part. When I wondered about achievable and realistic strategies for maintaining my personal and professional relationships, I leveraged the call-to-action portion of the reflection. I identified someone who was already doing what I was attempting and scheduled a meeting with her.

The self-reflection process creates places to look inside, uncover (rediscover) the connective elements between who we are individually, how we arrived at this space today, and what we feel called to do next. Not every reflection I wrote during that first graduate course, or the reflections I write now for that matter, are polished, shining examples of a complete reflection; however, what is just as true today for me, and I suspect will be for you as you flex your self-reflection muscles, is the intentional investment in moving through an outlined and defined system for reflection provides pathways and possibilities not previously seen or realized. Self-agency becomes possible and probable through the personal power that emerges through self-reflection.

There are three straightforward mantras around the ideology of practicing self-reflection. The disciplined act of developing self-reflection skills and capabilities only requires three non-negotiables for you, the practitioner:

1. Keep practicing.
2. Keep it real.
3. Keep it honest.

The first non-negotiable is a reminder: discipline > motivation. When reflecting feels difficult or uncomfortable, keep practicing. The topic, the "what" of the reflection, needs to be real for you, not a topic you think you *ought to be* reflecting about, or what someone else might be reflecting about. Just as important is the reminder of the third non-negotiable: how you respond, how you connect, *or* how you do not connect needs to be honest to who you are at this point of your journey.

Practice. Keep it real and keep it honest. Do not clean up the truth, your truth. There is no need for a polished reflection. An authentic self-reflection connects to your identity, describes connections to your beliefs/values/non-negotiables, and is truly only written for your personal discovery.

The deliberate practice of self-reflection is embedded in the ongoing commitment to growth and development. The intentional and purposeful attention to self-reflection creates pathways weaving through personal agency to uncover and discover biases. Discovering personal biases might feel daunting. You can make the choice to push past the weight of previously unknown biases and use those feelings as fuel for the call-to-action section of the reflective practice. Determination spurs momentum, and vice versa. Consider the two positions: reflection to cause a movement, and reflection because of a movement; which of the two self-reflection places is your starting point?

Practice implementing the four steps of the written reflection process detailed in this chapter, here.

Name!

Identify a recent circumstance or situation which caused you to pause, either in the moment, or following the circumstance. Maybe this is a conversation or exchange with a colleague, a neighbor, or a student.

Name it:_____

Connect!

Unpack and analyze the circumstances; understand the connections. What are the existing connections to your current understanding, values, intentions? Do connections exist with this topic and your role(s) responsibility? What might be a new connection or set of connections that create opportunities for deeper understanding? What are the implications if no further action is taken? What are the growth implications for self and others? Why does this circumstance matter to you and/or others?

_____
_____
_____
_____

Learn!

This section of the reflection asks and answers all four learning layers questions in relation to the topic and connections of section two. Learning is a requisite to moving forward as a reflective practitioner. Focus on self in response to each of the following:

What am I learning? Unlearning? Relearning? Resisting learning?

Reminder, this section of the reflective process specifically focuses on taking ownership of personal learning.

_____
_____
_____
_____

Do!

This is the action phase of the reflective cycle. Momentum is established and fueled by hope-filled purpose in the creation of next steps. This is the stage of the reflective process where self-agency is realized. The fourth section of the Reflective process is solidified with goal setting that includes progress monitoring. Describe your next steps, specifically considering and naming time, people, and resources.

What did the Connect and Learn sections of this reflection stir within? Reminder, in this section name how will you hold yourself able, capable, and accountable.

_____
_____
_____
_____

"Without reflection, we go blindly on our way, creating more unintended consequences, and failing to achieve anything useful." Margaret J. Wheatley

Chapter Takeaways

As you consider the two positions: reflection to cause a movement, and reflection because of a movement, are you currently situated in one location more than the other? Your position is where self-reflection begins.

Seek personal clarity and understanding of your life experiences that supported your current place in the world. The learning continuum is not intended to be a perfect line; personal progress is the goal.

6 Hope Is a Verb

Hope is active, not passive.

In early 2014, I was lucky enough to be in the audience with other educational leaders when Dr. Shane Lopez, author of *Making Hope Happen* (2013) spoke on the contagious truth of hope. Following the presentation, I personally, albeit briefly, spoke with Dr. Lopez. The unexpected joy from the conversation was a direct response to my lived experiences, including, then and now, a necessity to guard my hope from those who choose to weaponize it as a sign of weakness. A line from Lopez's book I revisit and find myself sharing with others often is, "How we hope determines how well we live our lives" (2013, 9).

Some people view hope as impractical and have not developed a personal understanding of how present hope is in their lives. Those who fail to see the benefits of choosing hope are also unlikely to recognize the existence of hope in their personal decision-making processes. That missing perspective does not make hope any less real and measurable. When a steady downpour of rain hinders the view out the window, does the obscured view mean the outside world ceases to exist? Of course not. Hope is tomorrow's currency, today; hope-filled people know and understand the value-centered principle of hope exists.

The innate ability to forecast potential outcomes, consider alternate plans, and set goals for the future are underpinned in the principles of hope. When it comes to the human behavior of forward thinking, and the agency of goal setting, hope is the foundation. My hope research, explored in Part II, highlights the core components of hope-filled adults with intersecting identities and dimensions of diversity. Reminder, the working definition of hope applied throughout this work is offered in the opening *At a Glance* section of this book. Throughout your reading, have you begun bridging hope's disciplined thinking and way of believing with your own reflective skill development and disposition? Where are you on the hope-filled continuum of development? How do you know?

Hope-filled vision is the ability to see beyond current circumstances and perceptions. Some of the psychological underpinnings associated with how one feels about self and changeable circumstances are tied to the extent one holds hope-filled thoughts. Any efficacious work on hope includes at least some findings by hope researcher, C. R. Snyder.

In the *Handbook of Hope* (Snyder 2000), the sophisticated psychology of hope stands on the solid footing of willpower and waypower. Individuals knowing, understanding, and acting on the momentum only possible with hope. Snyder's (2000) research finds hope is a mainstay of mindsets for some people by the age of twenty years. Without other longitudinal studies at the time, following the same group of people measuring hope throughout their lives, Snyder's in-depth study offers a significant cross-sectional view of the presence of hope across cultures, genders, and age groups.

Hope creates hope. Hope is the necessary ingredient for the heart and hard work of building equity-centered communities, regardless of role or title. "Complex work requires hope" (Arzonetti Hite and Donohoo 2021, 56). Each year, organizations across the globe conduct surveys to measure hope in individuals as young as fifth grade. In fact, for more than four decades, the Gallup Organization has gathered insights and perspectives from over six million students. Levels of hope and indicators of the likelihood of factors which positively contribute to hopeful communities are readily available information people can choose to seek, gather, pay attention to, and invest in for greater impact within and for community building.

Hope lives within any organization or community when there is a positive expectation that a mission or vision will be met collectively (Fry 2003).

In Part I of this work, I referenced interactions with various groups of students, undergraduate and graduate, specifically around the research for this book. In late fall of 2022, I first presented on the topic of culturally proficient leaders creating communities of belonging and hope at a national conference for educators and business leaders, regardless of position.

Session attendees included teacher leaders, education and industry program directors, city planners, board of education members, as well as educational district-level administrative leaders from across the United States, Canada, and Australia. Room capacity was met at just over 120 participants. The energy and focus of the room, filled with educators and those directly connected to community systems, served as its own data point and indication of topic interest.

Over the course of two years, I sought and received opportunities to present in similar national and regional gatherings on the topics of creating communities of belonging and hope. The definitional data of belonging and hope gathered and analyzed for this research are results from national and regional conferences in places like Denver, Colorado, Des Moines, Iowa, Austin, Texas, and Washington DC, offered by people from across the globe who intentionally chose to attend a conference session focused on belonging and hope.

The whole, vulnerable, insightful, open-responses sessions in which participants provided individually-held working definitions of belonging and hope serve as bedrocks for this work. The analysis and transformation of the qualitative data into manageable and meaningful thematic points included in this final section of the book are the action-based results indicating the value of self-reflection.

Constantly guiding the qualitative data-sleuthing focus of this research was the truth that each data point represents an individual and their perceptions around belonging and hope. The personal and direct role of the data points gathered and analyzed was honored with the strength qualitative data provides. The conclusions and identified themes represent the guaranteed validity of each human experience.

Submitting presentation proposals for national conferences with a subject line including belonging and hope became a sort of personal case study for me. Would conference organizers find the topics relevant and enticing enough for prospective participants? Once selected to present at each event, I wondered, up to the hour preceding each session, if conference attendees would be interested enough to attend a discussion clearly rooted in the personal action of creating and sustaining communities of belonging and hope.

Each time the session room filled with people, I found myself unable to begin the conversation in any way other than thanking the attendees for choosing a session with belonging and hope in the title. I named and leveraged the truth in the room; the filled spaces demonstrated a shared desire to create positive, equity-centered communities, regardless of geographic residence, levels of education, or the countless other dimensions of human reality.

I named session attendees as fellow Belonging and Hope Makers, pointing out, regardless of role, home region, or varied lived experiences, we *chose* to come together around equity-centered communities of belonging and hope; the same topics not always evident in social media posts and the media.

News reports and social media memes are easy enough to find, highlighting the fractured state and ills of the educational settings and communities in general. Yet, the conference rooms full of educational practitioners and industry leaders choosing to attend a session title naming the attention and intention of moving forward together demonstrate unity rather than separation in the field of education, in businesses, neighborhoods, and in homes.

Providing an opportunity for audience members to share motivations for attending the sessions also allowed the researcher in me to gather data. Participation in the digital Q/A opportunities throughout the session was voluntary and required a basic understanding of how to activate a link via QR code.

The session-opening verbal prompts I offered as a way of participation encouragement during the response-seeking portions of the session were the only external motivators offered to elicit response submissions. At times, I noticed within small groups, one person would submit a response on behalf of a pair or trio.

As I sought to understand the personal, and professional, reasons for attending a conference session focused on belonging and hope, the prompt also created an opportunity for the people in the room to connect with the topics at the onset of our time together. Session attendees responded to the initial prompt with goals including creating, increasing, and/or finding ways to build school and workplace cultures as communities of belonging.

Table 6.1 presents some session participants' responses to the prompt, "What is your role and a goal you have for attending today's session?" Table 6.1 is an authentic data set sampling, providing a glimpse of representation details around professional role/title and session attendance purpose, generally depicting individuals who attended any one of my conference sessions, regardless of location. Do you see glimpses of yourself in any of the attendees' shared descriptions?

Each time, over the course of two years, as I presented on this book's topic at national and regional conferences, I sought the same "purpose data." Curiosity

Table 6.1 Sample: Purpose Data

Program Director of Strategic Partnerships for Student Success at an education service district in Oregon (USA). The goal is to learn more about culturally proficient leadership and steps to create this environment.	I work at a State University to create a pipeline of equity-centered principals for public schools. My goal is to develop skills in invitation and disruption for change.	Local government Program Manager: Behavioral health, special education, and child welfare. Goals: listen, learn, practice skills, bring it back and move it forward.
I am an assistant principal in Colorado (USA). My goal is to learn all I can to be that change agent needed to support staff and students of color.	International Baccalaureate Program Coordinator, Education Leadership Student: To learn more about ways in which I can create spaces where all people feel valued, respected, and understood.	Local government Program Manager: Behavioral health, special education, and child welfare. Goals: listen, learn, practice skills, bring it back and move it forward.
I am the Director of Continuous Improvement in the Superintendent's Office. My goal is to continue to strengthen my knowledge and tools for engaging in and supporting racial equity work in my district.	Executive Director for Early Childhood- my hope is to learn more about what tools I could use in my role to assist families, children, and my colleagues.	I am a school board member from just north of Chicago (USA). I also work with school districts to use communications and community engagement to support and advance their equity work.
Executive Director of the American Indian Culture District in a large CA city (USA). I'm here to listen, learn, and learn about new tools to create positive change.	School counselor for a public-school magnet program. We tend to struggle to keep BIPOC and low SES students to feel like they belong with us and in our program. We need to work harder on building community.	University Professor- Learning more about building belonging with my pre-service teachers and modeling belonging with their future students.

Table 6.1 (Continued)

I am the School Board Vice President in my district in Wisconsin (USA). In WI there is very little development for board members in equity, so trying to learn.	Superintendent of three school districts! Looking to gain some knowledge and share it back in the districts I serve.	Assistant Superintendent of a school district in Oregon (USA). I am here to deepen my commitment to change.	Mental health therapist in schools and was drawn to the word HOPE in the title of the session!
Elementary School Principal San Francisco Bay Area (USA) I'm here to be present, mindful of my privileges as a white man, and grow.	Assistant Principal at a charter school in New York state (USA). My goal is to learn and engage in how we can make cultural proficiency actionable for us as leaders.	Director of Student Support- gain an understanding of my role in broken systems and how to bring multiple perspectives into educational practices.	Latina primary reading resource teacher, Maryland (USA). My goal is to continue to build muscle as a leader in Equity so I can be an agent for change.
In HR and want to take back strategies to support our goals of creating communities of belonging within our employee community.	I hope to find more ways to encourage others to find the value in creating systems of belonging for the communities we serve.	Superintendent- looking to add tools to my toolbox for this great work in our district.	I am the Director of Human Resource, and my hope is to listen and learn how I can be a change agent in my role.

Note: Identifying descriptors are redacted for participants' anonymity.

about others who also prioritized equity-centered communities of belonging and hope allowed the responses of session attendees to weave a tapestry of humanity within the pages of this book. The qualitative data gathered is situated within the broader work of community building and self-reflection, providing context and adding meaning to the purpose of this writing. The variety of people, with varied backgrounds and professional roles, seeking to know more about some of the elements related to transformational change through the equity-centered lens of belonging and hope are likely also *Change Demanders*.

"No change is possible without hope. No movement is possible without hope" (Angela Davis 2022).

A commitment to seeking and knowing people on an individual level is part of an equity-valuing system. When systems are structured and restructured to intentionally marginalize, minoritize, and exclude individuals or groups, historically centered members of the dominant culture are the benefactors. The opposite is not true.

To more accurately discern system benefactors, be courageous enough to follow the *Who Trail*. Change Demanders ask the questions others cannot or are not asking.

Who Trail

- → *Who* built the system?
- → *Who* decided who the system architects would be?
- → *Whose* voice, ideas, and input were a part of the system design?
- → *Who* was considered during system construction, piloting, and testing?
- → *Who* was excluded, overtly or subtly?
- → *Who* was intentionally included in the cost/benefit analysis of the system's construction, and who was intentionally excluded?

Systems are built intentionally or by default, and systems are maintained intentionally or by default. Questioning how the system was built, for what purposes, and *who* is served by the system creates opportunities for introspection and reflection about one's own role within the system. This reflective practice is an example of owning one's connection, responsibility, and impact within a particular system or community.

The will, skill, and personal accountability go hand in hand with intellectual wrestling around the concepts of systems development and systems over time. Objectively following the *Who Trail* requires personal cognitive strength and a willingness to uncover uncomfortable truths about self or the organizations you are a part of.

The capability to realize systems solidly built with advantages for some and divisive disadvantages for others may be especially challenging for individuals whose role responsibilities include maintaining those same systems. The introspective heavy lifting of recognizing that while the work *seems* well-intended, it is in fact carrying-on systemic exclusions requires a personally persistent openness.

During a professional conversation on systemic privileges and biases, a titled leader in education recently asked, "What evidence do you have that if systems were built by people not usually at the table the outcomes would be better? What evidence is there the results would be any better?" The reflexive, automatic response from a few colleagues was, "Better for whom?" A more objective response to the "what evidence" question is that the scales of social justice are tipped toward equity-centered solutions and systems renovation with the weight of diverse perspectives. When data is missing, primary source data, that is firsthand perspectives unfiltered from others' interpretation, how can a comprehensive, equity-centered system be built? Regularly challenge yourself to consider a system, a procedure, a result from someone else's comfort zone, not from the safety of your own comfort zone. I refer to this process as the Humble Courage Exercise. Admitting to a blind spot, an unconscious bias, or an undeveloped area around cultural proficiency, and then being courageous enough to do something about it is Humble Courage.

The Humble Courage Exercise requires specificity on both parts of the process. This is another space and place where the comfortably numb center survives and thrives on ambiguity and highly generalized next steps, such as "I will have more conversations with people whose lived experiences do not match mine." Where is the sticking point in that call to action? What personal system of accountability and capability exists in the vagueness of the "more conversations" statement? How will you set yourself up for success as you reflect and create personal opportunities for growth?

A personal commitment to engaged self-awareness is maintained only with humility and curiosity. Right-sizing our lived experiences is not about being right but rather about the advancement of humanity with an equity-valued lens. Humbly admitting to blind spots in understanding another's lived experience does not lessen your own. The willingness to openly receive another's lived experience requires removing yourself from the center of the story being shared.

De-centering yourself is especially tricky when, by doing so, you fear your individual story will carry less value. When individual lived experiences are combined with others' who share the value of equity-centered community building, we create a robust, textured, colorful tapestry. Each individual thread is as strong as the one next to it. Fraying is impossible when no one is picking at the edges or trying to pull apart the threads.

Following is a nudge to continue your self-reflection journey. Cultivate your personal will and skill development, daring to discover pressure points of undermined systems' awareness.

Pause and Process

As you read the questions associated with the "who" trail on the previous pages, what are some of your initial reactions?

_____
_____
_____
_____

Identify one system you are a part of by choice and/or intentionality.

_____

Who are the "named" benefactors of the system you identified above? (individuals/groups)

_____
_____
_____
_____

Who does not benefit and who may be at a disadvantage because of the system? (individuals/groups)

_____
_____
_____
_____
_____
_____

Who is responsible for monitoring and evaluating the effectiveness of the system? And how are those evaluation processes communicated to people in and out of the system?

_____
_____
_____
_____
_____
_____

Who has access to the system-effectiveness data? Who decides?

_____
_____
_____
_____
_____
_____

What do *you* consider your connection to and responsibility within the system?

_____
_____
_____
_____
_____
_____
_____

What are the incentives (tangible and intangible) to maintaining the current system?

_____
_____
_____
_____
_____

What questions do you have now and where will you start looking for answers?

_____
_____
_____
_____
_____
_____
_____

Chapter Takeaways

Consider your hope-filled mindset. When does hope thrive in you? What does *sharing hope* mean for you? Are there instances or places when you feel instinctively compelled to guard your hope?

Humble courage requires us to uncover blind spots and be courageous enough to move from self-awareness toward personal growth and development. What are your next steps toward a personal commitment fueled by humility and curiosity?

7 Community Building Is Capacity Building

May your choices reflect your hopes, not your fears. —Nelson Mandela

Imagine the potential for inclusive communities of belonging and hope when each member is evaluating the effectiveness of the system through the lens of each lived experience, not just one's own vantage point. The process of interrogating one's individual identity within a community, organization, or system, along with leaning into role responsibility, creates pockets of hope-filled opportunities.

Is role responsibility limiting the variety of lived experiences sought, shared, and valued within the system, organization, or community? Without investing in the process of critical inquiry and asking questions, how will you know and understand the shields of a system being wielded, intentionally or unintentionally?

When reflection leads to uncovering and discovering personal membership within a system or community, any bias unconsciously or selectively held is brought into the light. Uncovering a personally held subconscious bias is the first step toward removing the actions that continue upholding the bias structure. Embracing the complexity around the multiple dimensions of diversity that are humans' reality is powerful fuel for equity-centered community building.

If someone is not willing to measure the distance from their own understanding and lived experience to that of the person standing farthest away, how much of the individual's knowing and understanding is based on evidence-based truth, and how much is held together by intricately woven systems of exclusion? It seems unlikely and highly improbable to have a productive conversation about equity-centered communities of belonging and hope without unpacking one's own membership and role responsibilities within chosen communities.

In late 2023, during an opportunity to present at a national conference on this book's topics, I stood at the front of the room, introducing myself by name and intention, inviting participants to do the same at the twenty tables of five or six people each. Valuing each person's role in the room and attempting to create a safe space for conversations rooted in self-reflection, I asked for a few volunteers willing to share personal reasons for attending the session.

I will not forget the stories and lived experiences shared by the people in the room, specifically two workshop participants. Seated together at a table in the middle of the room, one wearing a light blue Hijab and the other a deep brown Hijab, the two women shared frightening encounters in stores, hotels, and on the streets. The courageous women offered terror-filled lived experiences and wondered about the possibility of authentically holding equity-centered conversations about communities of belonging and hope when neither seldom felt valued, a sense of belonging or hopeful.

Each woman shared harrowing experiences of fearing for personal safety and the safety of their families following the 2016 US presidential election. The two told of being taunted and jeered at an airport, malls, and on the subways for wearing a Hijab.

The woman in a deep brown Hijab looked around the room, locking eyes with me as she shared a story of her middle-school-aged son being bullied and physically assaulted more than once at school for his religious beliefs within the last three years. She voiced deep mother's fear for two daughters in the year 2023 wearing Hijabs to school and in public spaces. Consciously, or unconsciously, touching the dark silk on her head as she spoke, her eyes conveying worry and uncertainty.

The other woman pleaded with each of us in the room to use whatever privilege we held in our local communities to stand up and speak out for equal protection under the law. With an elevated voice, she questioned how someone who looks like me, presumably a middle-class white woman, could "know" about her lived experience. At that moment, I responded with words you have already read in this book, "... by asking and believing."

The next day as I entered the crowded Austin, Texas airport, a privilege in itself, dressed casually in a sweatshirt, my mind's eye could not help seeing the two women from the day before, who bravely led a courageous conversation in a space full of strangers. The daring and strength displayed by the two women meant their shared lived experiences might form and shape future actions for each person in the room.

Truly "knowing" another's lived experience is not entirely possible for me, or you, or any of us; a truth boldly underscoring the real and necessary need for lived experiences, different from one's own, being sought, believed, and amplified. Creating equity-centered communities starts with each of us prioritizing the commitment to equity, belonging, and hope, especially those of us with social capital as members of the dominant culture.

"Dominator culture has tried to keep us all afraid, to make us choose safety instead of risk, sameness instead of diversity. Moving through that fear, finding out what connects us, reveling in our differences; this is the process that brings us closer, that gives us a world of shared values, of meaningful community" (Hooks 2003, 197).

McIntosh's 1989 work and studies around white privilege, Unpacking the Invisible Knapsack, survey participants identify the extent to which everyday life experiences are related to the individual's race. While the survey items could just as easily identify community inclusion for any number of personal traits, including gender identification, socio-economic status, and ethnicity, race is the starting point. All other "isms" in the United States fall in line behind racism, which upholds systems of oppression, known and unknown by all members of the community.

The social construct of race, with historical origins included in the US Colonial period beginning in the seventeenth century, separates humanity and creates a hierarchy based on physical characteristics, most prominently distinguished by an individual's skin color.

Reaching back to the seventeenth century, the social and cultural construct of race in the United States has been used to create divisions and as an intentional system of oppression. Racial identity is the starting point for uncovering bias in self, and institution, if one is focused on dismantling systems of oppression created by systemic social constructs. Race matters because racism matters. When racism is wholly dismantled, systems of oppression begin to fall for all.

In her 2014 dissent in *Schuette v. Coalition* to Defend Affirmative Action, the honorable Sonya Sotomayor, Supreme Court Justice, reminded, "Race matters. Race matters in part because of the long history of racial minorities being denied access to the political process. . . . Race also matters because of the persistent racial inequality in society. This refusal to accept the stark reality that race matters is regrettable."

Self-reflection creates space for perception shifts, provoking mindfulness and curiosity in place of judgment. Having differences among and between another person is not a reason for separation; individually held *judgment* about human differences is where the divide among people *grows wider*. Acknowledging differences is not an admission of bias. What one does or does not do regarding differences between self and another person connects the dots between inclusive living and sharing spaces *or* maintaining biases.

Are you able to identify a point, if such exists, when someone in your life silenced your curiosity about a known or potential difference between you and another? Have you, through the lens of "good intentions," silenced a thought, a wondering, or a conversation to avoid naming a difference? Have you experienced an opposite scenario? What worked? What did not go well? Why?

The Fallacy of Conditional Inclusion

Collaborating and meeting with a variety of people connected to PK-20+ education means I have been a part of learning environments when someone declares *inclusion* as part of their individually held beliefs, and yet, when faced with someone whose ideals appear to be on the other end of the continuum, rather than demonstrating active inclusion, exclusion (emotional, physical, intellectual) occurs. The inclusion illusion is performative, Virtue Signaling, not substantive, and authentic inclusion.

Conditional inclusion is a glossed over, in varying degrees, version of authentic inclusion. The reflexive response of excluding someone or a segment of the population because one does not agree with their lifestyle or personal choices is an example of conditional inclusion. Thereby, creating a fallacy of owning an inclusion values set for self. The internal dialogue included with conditional inclusion might sound something like "I include you as long as your actions, thoughts, or opinions more closely match or mirror mine," or "I include you in this space with limitations."

Diversity of thought, opinions, viewpoints, and perspectives is part of the human experience. In truth, the dimensions of diversity layers we are each composed of are too numerous to count. Reflective practices do not wash away individual characteristics, purposes, or missions. Rather, the opposite is true. Self-reflection is a mindful inquiry toward seeing, knowing, and understanding yourself beyond the overt and casually known layers.

The systematic and intentional process of self-reflection creates a more robust understanding of oneself, one's place in the world, and personal capabilities. Creating inclusive communities of belonging and hope is not a denial of differences in human experiences; these communities celebrate and amplify differences in each other.

"What you reflect on determines what you will learn" (Maxwell 2019).

Authentic reflection requires trust in self, in the process, and in the potential of the unknown outcome because of reflecting. Trusting yourself to leverage reflective practices is connected to the extent to which you believe in the capacity for self-growth and your self-determined *need* to grow in a particular area or on a particular topic.

Asking yourself tough questions related to past, current, and future actions, and then fully sitting with truthful answers are reflective practitioners' foundational building blocks. I did not just stumble into an awareness that the "colorblind" thinking and responses I carried during my interview for a teaching position in the early 1990s were examples of whitewashing. I wrestled with what I thought I knew by leaning into the reflective process in the Four Stages of Learning©. I needed to unlearn systemic whiteness masked as benevolence to understand erasing one's racial identity is not a pathway to creating communities of belonging.

The willingness and capability to ask challenging questions of oneself, before asking others, is an example of a reflective practitioner's skill; this is referred to as the inside/outside work. We ask and answer the questions for ourselves before turning outward and asking the same of the systems or people we serve. *Asking* the difficult and/or *discomfort-causing* questions as part of intentional self-assessment is the first step, followed by honestly *answering* the same questions as the action-causing next step. Which questions are you avoiding asking yourself? How do you know? Which questions do you automatically intellectualize or rationalize from a "safe" distance?

The personal armor each of us wears provides a shield from external aggressors or internal investigations. And, at times, our personal armor creates an impenetrable shell for both self and others. Consider a circumstance when you were on the receiving end of faux inclusion, or an instance when you offered conditional inclusion to someone else. The ability to slip on personal armor is innate for self-preservation and not necessarily always linked to positive connections.

Lean into the chance to unpack personally held social construct understandings and refrain from slipping on personal armor. Which responses to questions about racial identity, gender, social and cultural construction, and community membership do you reluctantly hold or shield yourself and others from knowing?

The following Pause and Process invites you to consider personal identities held and assigned by self/others. Lean into this chance to have a courageous conversation with yourself. If you are not willing to ask and answer the questions for yourself, is it realistic to expect others to answer?

Pause and Process

1. How do you identify ethnically and racially?

   _____
   _____
   _____
   _____
   _____
   _____

2. When was the last time you engaged in a conversation about race and ethnicity with someone who shares your identity? Describe your comfort level and the depth of the conversation.

   _____
   _____
   _____
   _____
   _____
   _____

3. When did you last engage in a conversation about race and ethnicity with someone whose identity does not match yours? Describe your comfort level and the depth of the conversation.

4. As you began processing questions 1–3 above, what was your internal level of comfort? Describe your initial feelings and thoughts.

5. What are your first, next steps in identifying cultural and societal constructs defining "who" you are?

After thinking through your reflective responses to the first set of conditions for the previous Pause and Process, stay in the processing mode and replace "ethnically and racially" with other constructs like gender, sexual orientation, religious and socio-political identities, or cultural identities.

What do you notice about your initial responses? Is one set of identification qualifiers more or less difficult for you to personally consider? Is there an identification qualifier you sense personal resistance around applying the pause and process framework? If you answered *yes* or *maybe* to either of the previous two questions, there is a personal call to action for you just under the surface.

Culturally proficient development includes owning and growing through language use and language leveraging. Vague terms and word choices are more easily manipulated by those individuals and groups who benefit from positions within the community, either by title or privilege-based roles. When words used in and out of a community carry different meanings or hold ambiguous understanding, the group benefiting from systems of privilege exploits the language.

Accepting the call to expand individual word choice and degrees of understanding pushes back on the groundless power established by limiting language. Language holds the power to refine, build, and disrupt cycles built on *power over*, and create personal systems of accountability built on *power to*.

Look no further than 2023 when book bans in public library systems across the United States became a part of public forums and town hall meetings. The American Library Association (2024)[1] reports book bans rose by 92 percent in 2023 in comparison to previous years. The social and political noise around indoctrinating young children and children from the centered class is able to take hold not only because of fear-mongering but also because of the lack of common definitions for terms such as culturally proficient and culturally responsive.

Neither of the phrases culturally proficient and culturally responsive is connected to the law school study of critical race theory, and yet, in the United States, all three phrases are often spun together in a tangled web enveloping community and public education spaces, garnering support for agendas pushed by those who certainly benefit from the marginalization of other individuals and communities.

In early 2024, I was fortunate to accept a dinner invitation welcoming a scholar and national equity, inclusion, and diversity presenter to the area. Among the small group of reception attendees were long-standing university professors, an undergraduate student leader, higher education staff, and others invested in what connects and disconnects humans. A natural progression of the conversation swayed toward which words were moving in and out of the current zeitgeist around equity, inclusion, and diversity, and which words have become weaponized.

Suddenly, many of the words and phrases found in the Working Definitions section of this book were bantered around as potentially fading from popularity or as tinder for division. No one at the table registered surprise at the word choice tug of war playing out politically and socially. A lack of common working definitions equates to a lack of focus on what is really at stake in any movement, and especially in the heart and hard work of creating equity-centered communities of belonging and hope.

Chapter Takeaways

This chapter reinforces the dynamics of proactive community building, asking each of us to reflect on individual choices around seeking to know and honor others' life experiences. Explore the fallacy of conditional inclusion in your current reality.

Incomplete understanding and uncertain definitions for culturally responsive and culturally proficient leading create divisive opportunities for members of the dominant culture.

Are there words and phrases used in your social circles, at work, at home, or on social media you may not have a fully formed, bias-free understanding of?

Is establishing clarity around particular words, ideas, or concepts a call to action for you?

Note

1 https://www.google.com/url?q=https://www.ala.org/news/mediapresscenter/presskits/surge-book-challenges-press-kit&sa=D&source=docs&ust=1729042300269476&usg=AOvVaw1XMQX0y4DoZaBGWCtKqPjS

Part II
The Sweet Spot of Belonging and Hope

8 The People-Centered Promise

The last section of this book unpacks the qualitative data, the anchor of this research on belonging and hope collected over two years. If reading the previous sentence caused your eyes to glaze over at seeing a section focused on data, here is a reminder: each data point represents a person.

On the other hand, if reading the first sentence of this chapter fueled you to read faster, welcome. *Continuous improvement* for self, organizations, systems, and communities is, in part, nestled securely in *understanding the power of knowing individual and collective perspectives*.

My commitment to honoring the integrity and validity of the qualitative data collected throughout this research is as strong as the trust placed in me by all the participants who provided narrative responses with sincerity and authenticity. Qualitative research is the quest to investigate social conditions and human behaviors through non-numerical data sets.

The initial data analysis was based on the *location context*—where the data was gathered. This step included isolating data sets based on the regional and/or national conference sources. The second tier of data analysis focused on larger sets related to individual strand data types. Themes were continuously and consistently refined with the qualitative researcher's method of constant comparison (Glaser and Strauss 1967).

As previously mentioned, my presentations on equity-centered communities of belonging and hope at various locations across the United States included gathering data from a variety of people who traveled to three regions (southern, eastern, western) and the center of the United States to attend national and regional conferences. Each session included individuals from various professional community roles, as well as positions within the education system.

The variety of professional pursuits in Table 6.1 demonstrates a broad human interest in inclusivity, belonging, and hope across various levels and types of industry and educational institutions. As a planned segment of my presentations and continued research for this book, gathering what I refer to as *Purpose* data from individuals attending a session focused on creating communities of belonging and hope was incorporated into the beginning of each session. In other words, the *Purpose* data represents session-goers' *why* for attending.

After analyzing the qualitative data across multiple perspectives, I held a keen awareness for honoring the "voices" in the shared responses, serving as a primary research protocol. Serving as the data sets caretaker is exhilarating and daunting. The researcher's responsibility to each data point, filter-free, is crucial. Each session attendee entrusted me with personal definitions and purpose statements, candidly offered. The weight of the data sets in my care felt, at times, equal measures overwhelming and exhilarating—and both feelings equally propelled me to the finish line of this book.

As previously highlighted, each data point represents an individual. A qualitative researcher's due diligence includes creating a platform for the authenticity of the collected data to paint a picture. Three prevailing *Purpose* data themes emerged from the responses of people who chose to attend conference sessions focused on this book's topics.

> The qualitative data themes for the *Purpose* data set:
> - Commitment to Inclusivity;
> - Strengthening Leadership;
> - Community Building and Inspiration.

Commitment to Inclusivity

The *Purpose* data gathered from people attending my sessions focused on creating equity-centered communities of belonging and hope named a desire to create more inclusive environments and more inviting school and work communities while ensuring each person feels they belong. The people-centered promise underneath this layer of data is a core element of humanity, what anthropological researchers identify as human beings' innate desire to be *in community* together.

During a 2022 interview for *Educational Psychology Review* with noted belonging researchers Baumeister and Leary, Leary stated, "once researchers began to examine topics related to belonging and acceptance, they saw the effect of this motive everywhere. No matter what else people may be doing, they seem to keep an eye on their connections with other people" (2022, 1150).

The *Purpose* data set indicates an emphasis on prioritizing inclusivity and belonging. Inclusive communities require inclusive practices. Inclusive communities are spaces and places that cultivate possibilities. Inclusive communities are complicated and collaborative, often at the same time, because people are complicated and collaborative. It is impossible to talk about or plan to build authentic communities without first knowing and validating the personhood of members.

The dynamics of systems fused together as inclusive communities establish relational trust, not despite differences, rather because of the multitude of dimensions each person carries across race, socio-economic status, gender, language, religion, ability, immigration status, sexuality, geographical location, and other identities owned by individuals.

Several *Purpose* data respondents sought innovative ideas, tools, tips, and strategies to take back to teams or implement in personal and professional settings. People attended the sessions seeking tangible takeaways. Looking for plausible and realistic next steps aimed at unifying organizations and creating inclusive environments starts with interrogating current truths of self and systems in place. Choosing to walk through a door framed with words like culturally responsive leadership and equity-centered spaces points to the mindfulness and curiosity detailed in previous chapters, serving as cornerstones of self-reflection.

Discussion topics around enhancing group cohesion and home/work environments, with a laser-like focus on self and others' well-being, surged through participants' opening comments during small group table conversations. The qualitative researcher in me observed the dynamics between session-goers who attended alone, in pairs, and in small work groups.

Context matters: In the post-2019 pandemic era, when people began gathering again at large-venue conferences, the fact each session titled with words including equity-centered, belonging, and hope was filled with people from across the United States and neighboring countries was satisfying and promising.

As a human and a researcher who instinctively gathers perception data in nearly every room I enter, the thoughtful curiosity on display in the session rooms focused on equity, belonging, and hope confirmed my solidly held belief in the positive perseverance of the collective human spirit—despite the ongoing political atrocities occurring in the United States and across the globe.

Strengthening Leadership

A significant number of session respondents held titled leadership positions within community or governmental agencies and in education (such as principals, directors, or central office administrators). The data theme associated with enhancing personally held leadership skills identified a specific interest in becoming more culturally proficient. The vibrancy associated with culturally proficient leadership is socially, academically, and interpersonally framed around amplifying the value of each individual's lived experience within the organization or community. How? What does this look like, sound like, and include? Leading through the lens of belonging and hope requires knowing and understanding *who you are* as a dispositional leader and *whom you are serving*.

Culturally responsive leadership is active. Examining common practices, established policies, and routine procedures through the equity-value lens is the first step in challenging the status quo. When you challenge the status quo, you choose to think against the grain. Rejecting the status quo first requires actually knowing the state of routines and procedures not serving all members with an equity-centered lens.

Consider someone else's status quo, in addition to your own. What are the parallels and separate distinctions between multiple views of *more of the same*? Establishing operational strategies that seek to know the cultures of the people being served involves intentional steps such as neighborhood and community audits, highlighting historical context with present-day realities. Boosting understanding for self and others enhances culturally proficient leadership by empowering all voices, especially the voices and perspectives of people who are marginalized; the same people who are routinely expected to exist in the margins while simultaneously supporting dominant culture-centered practices. Validating lived experiences leads to empowerment (Ladson-Billings 2009).

Personal assessment through self-reflection determines your readiness and capabilities centered on cultural proficiency. This is where personal identity work comes in. As you read the first two of three purpose data points: *Commitment to Inclusivity* and *Strengthening Leadership*, where did you find yourself nodding in confirmed agreement or frowning in confusion or resistance?

Leverage the Four Stages of Learning© and check in with yourself in relation to ideas and concepts you encountered in this section of the reading:

What are you learning about yourself?

_____
_____
_____
_____

What are you *re*learning about yourself?

_____
_____
_____
_____

What are you *un*learning about yourself?

_____
_____
_____
_____

What are you *resisting* learning about yourself?

_____
_____
_____
_____

Community Building and Inspiration

Common expressions of goals centered on creating a positive community, reigniting the community, or making schools and organizations a welcoming and connected place were repeatedly offered in the Purpose data set. A qualitative data theme centered on community building and inspiration represents a culture-building commitment. This call to action confronts the illusion of inclusion and is instead the point of courageous transitions for leaders, regardless of position, who hold privileges not accessible by all. When people are excluded and limited, so are ideas.

Community building requires architects and builders to maximize the potential for creative, inclusive, and innovative problem-solving. The blueprints of inspired, equity-centered communities are distinguishable from the status quo by the vital components represented through diversity of experiences, thoughts, perspectives, and social identities. Valuing and supporting the well-being of each community member cannot be superficial or performative; the facade of a hollow community cannot withstand the eventual storms naturally occurring during phases of group development (Tuckman 1965).

Teammates' and colleagues' verbal back and forth, at times turbulent, Tuckman's team confirmed, are exactly the points where teams and groups identify where they stand individually *and* collectively. In culture-building processes, finding common ground for forward momentum toward continuous improvement happens after the storm, because of the storm. A commitment to community building is a commitment to continuous improvement.

The single focus of big-data myopia, which is primarily accessing and leveraging the large-scale assessment data points generated by long-standing, centrically designed systems, perpetuates practices, policies, and systems already in place. Big-data myopia certainly nets the results the systems were intended to yield. New ways of being and doing happen only through intentional practice. Utilizing a comprehensive data gathering process with firsthand perspectives of people from all levels of the organization or community to identify the patterns and results, with an eyes wide open mindset, is part of the heart and hard work of equity-centered leadership, regardless of position.

Conversations among decision-makers at all levels of the organizational flow chart must move away from intellectual tropes like perfectionism and big-data myopia. Perfectionism freezes actions until we can "be certain" any changes or systems renovation are the right next steps. The question I hope you are automatically asking is, "The next right steps for who?" The immobilization tethered to intellectual perfectionism masks one of the direct complicities of time mechanisms decision-makers are called to see and release.

Resisting the fear of failure opens the doors to systems creation rooted in authentic inclusion and equity-centered communities of belonging. If you fear making mistakes, your focus is on self-protection, not personal growth. Embedded just below the surface of the words "let's make sure we have evidence this will work" are entrenched roots of the status quo. "Change is hard, and sustainable systemic improvement is tougher" (Arzonetti Hite and Donohoo 2021).

The data-sleuthing call to action includes identifying productive patterns where the organization and people of the organization stand engaged within multifaceted inclusive systems. The complete call to action also includes clearly identifying destructive patterns netting exclusion and "othering." Implement targeted strategies with laser-like focus on uncovering and discovering the *Who Trail* highlighted in Chapter 6.

In your neighborhood, community, and organizations, how are individuals' perspectives proactively sought? Notice the omission of the question around reactionary seeking in the previous question. Is positivity authentically evident via relational trust and integrity? What are the co-created formal and informal practices framed by individual dignity and validation? It is impossible to fully know what is working if we do not also know what is not working for each member of the organization, community, or team.

Shared power and partnerships through a vision of each member's equal value to the community become a measurable goal, pushing beyond random acts of inclusion toward equity-centered communities. Several session respondents' Purpose data responses mentioned the value of hope, either in terms of building communities of hope, enabling and building hope within others, or keeping all doors open for all students through hope.

A clear theme of seeking to *inspire hope* in colleagues, neighbors, family, and friends came forward in the Purpose data set. There is power and potential behind the call to action to *inspire hope* from session attendees in a variety of leadership roles. "hope is a combination of setting goals, having the tenacity and perseverance to pursue them, and believing in our own abilities" (Brown 2021, 240). So then, inspiring hope is embedded in the heart and hard work of culturally proficient leaders. Inspired hopefulness first comes from inside, as do other motivating factors driving the innovation grounded in sustaining equity-centered communities of belonging.

The three Purpose data themes: Commitment to Inclusivity; Strengthening Leadership; Community Building and Inspiration represent *why* individuals and/or work teams elected to attend a session focused on creating communities of hope and belonging.

Unpack and discover where you meet the Purpose data themes. In Chapter 5, the four-pronged Reflective process was explained, and you were encouraged to stretch your reflective muscles. The repeating, ongoing practice of a personal check-in is aimed at monitoring understanding and recognizing belief connections/disconnects with systems and circumstances. How much of your behavior is predictably connected to your level of discomfort when you confront a personal bias?

Each section of the reflective process includes built-in prompts to engage your thinking and levels of awareness; it is not necessary to respond to every prompt like short-answer test questions. Instead, leverage the prompts as personal thought-builders; once your reflective muscle kicks in, naturally develop that section of the Reflective Cycle. A couple of reminders for you: the four sections of the self-reflection framework are intended to build on one another, and the non-negotiables for you, as you develop your reflective skills, are:

1. Keep practicing.
2. Keep it real.
3. Keep it honest.

Name!

Identify which of the three Purpose data themes: Commitment to Inclusivity; Strengthening Leadership; Community Building and Inspiration is resonating with you, maybe because you have more questions than answers when you consider the theme, or because as you read about the three Purpose data themes you noticed an unexpected internal reaction.

Name it:

_____
_____
_____

Connect!

Consider the connections and disconnects to your known beliefs and ideas. Are there existing connections to your current understanding of community-building, values, intentions? Do connections exist with this topic and your role(s) responsibility? What are new connections or sets of connections creating opportunities for deeper understanding? What are the implications if no further action is taken; are there growth implications for self and others? Why does this circum*stance matter to you and/or others?*

_____
_____
_____
_____
_____
_____
_____
_____

Learn!

This section of the reflection asks and answers all four learning layers questions in relationship to your selected topic and the connections you identified in section two. Focus on your personal awareness in response to each of the following because this section of the reflective process specifically focuses on taking ownership of personal learning.

What am I learning? Unlearning? Relearning? Resisting learning?

_____
_____
_____
_____
_____
_____
_____
_____

Do!

This final, action phase of the reflective cycle establishes and is fueled by hope-filled purpose as you identify next steps. Include some possible progress monitoring opportunities as you describe your next steps. Specifically list timestamps for *personal accountability, people, and resources you will seek.*

_____
_____
_____
_____
_____
_____
_____
_____
_____
_____
_____
_____
_____

Chapter Takeaways

Culturally responsive leadership is active. Moving away from big-data myopia is required for those of us determined to serve communities with a culturally responsive lens. The singular focus on large-scale assessments designed to serve and meet the needs of dominant culture members freezes forward movement behind the mask of *waiting for the next right tool*. Do you have personal examples related to each of the Purpose data themes?

Commitment to Inclusivity

Strengthening Leadership

Community Building and Inspiration

9 The Essentialness of Belonging

Be the change you wish to see in the world.—Mahatma Gandhi

Belonging is not camouflaged in partial phases of reality. Belonging is when *who* you are and who *you* are, are the very fibers in the fabric of the community. There is an essentialness within the group held by each member, as multifaceted identities of each person are woven into an equity-centered community. Belonging is active and not negotiable.

Time and again, during the opening portions of the national and regional sessions focused on owning personal calls to action, engaged participants responded with certainty, and often with quickness, confirming they personally knew places and spaces where they belong *and* the circumstances when the opposite was true. Knowing what it feels like to *not* belong just as certainly, and as quickly, as identifying where belonging *does* exist, is in itself a call to action for decision-makers and leaders, regardless of position and organizational affiliation.

Can you name a place *you know you belong*? Now think of a time or circumstance when you knew you did *not belong*. Just as you know what an inclusive community of belonging feels like *and* does not feel like, rest assuredly, so too does the person sitting next to you on the train, standing in line at the grocery store, walking past you on the sidewalk, and entering your workplace after you on Monday morning. We are all seeking authentic connection through belonging and hope, as this research confirms.

The final chapters of this book offer a deeper look at the analyzed data around personally held definitions of belonging and hope, voluntarily provided by national and regional conference attendees—people who chose to attend sessions titled with belonging, hope, and equity-centered language. As you read, notice your personal process for connecting the dots between what the research confirms with your life experiences and backgrounds.

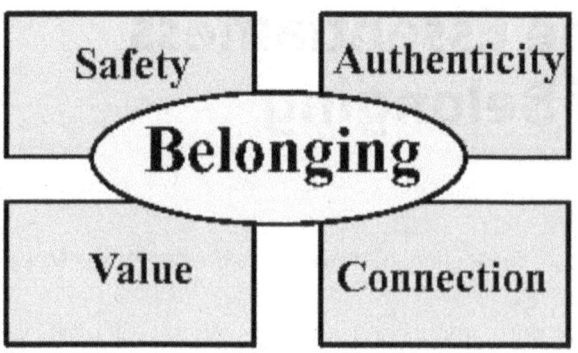

Figure 9.1 Belonging data themes. Perkins (2025).

The mental model for the qualitative themes for the Belonging data set (Figure 9.1).

As I poured over research participants' definitional data for belonging, clear themes and ideological truths emerged. The behavioral messages, both subtle and unmistakable, associated with the themes of this data set underscore how keenly aware most of us are when we belong *and* when we do not belong. And yet, when we are aware the factors associated with personal belonging are not present, the individual transformation of displaying the prevailing and expected behaviors, attitudes, and norms becomes acts of self-preservation. Masks for fitting in are worn to protect individual identities.

A reminder about the data-gathering process during my conference sessions titled around creating cultural proficiency and equity-centered communities of belonging and hope, a QR code linked session participants to a stand-alone data collection landing page. Intentionally, respondents were able to see and interact with one another's responses by offering a thumbs up/down or heart.

Each respondent voluntarily answered the following questions:

How do you define Belonging? What does Belonging mean to you?

Unpacking the emerging themes from the Belonging data set highlights participants' core human desire to be secure, needed, validated, and valued. As you read the four Belonging data set themes, note where you show up among the descriptors and places you would add to the theme.

Safety

The safety data theme includes both physical and emotional well-being. Knowing the environment is *safe* to be yourself is linked to personal authenticity. Participants' responses fused belonging with feelings of safety and comfort. Phrases like *safe place, comfortable in my skin,* and *feeling safe* point to the close ties of belonging to an individual's innate sense of security and ease.

The stability existing when bias-free spaces are built and sustained allows each of us to *be*, knowing we are *safe from rejection, judgment, and harm*. The association between belonging and feelings of safety is not altogether surprising and spotlights the foundational elements of relationship building. The relational layer of comfort is only possible when someone knows they are safe, physically and emotionally, both in the space and with the people also holding membership within the group or community.

Authenticity

Several responses anchor belonging to the ability to be one's true self. The *authenticity* data theme of Belonging is described with phrases like *Where I belong is where I can be my truest self* and *Belonging is when it is safe to stand out*. Belonging behavior patterns evolved out of authenticity and self-expression. Authenticity emerged from the data responses emphasizing the genuine essence of self as a key aspect of belonging. *I didn't have to hide any part of myself.*

The state of Belonging exists when you are *free to be your true, authentic self without fear of repercussions*. Statements like *being in a place where you can be your best self* and *seeing yourself, as you truly are, in a space that celebrates you* confirm belonging coincides with personally knowing and believing your individuality is known, seen, and validated. There is no reason to hide behind partial truths, concealed versions of yourself, or conform to others' norms and behaviors in equity-centered communities of belonging.

Showing up as your authentic self carries the *feeling of being welcome in a space where you are not all the same*, and yet, *all are respected and accepted*. The *authenticity* theme of the Belonging data set is defined as the capability and desire to share your vulnerabilities without backlash and insult, or as one respondent shared, belonging is *freedom to be a beautiful mess and 1. Accept myself for it and 2. Allow others to love me for it.*

Value

The individuals-as-assets mindset is laced throughout the Belonging data theme of *value*. Personal validation includes both feeling and knowing your existence in the group adds value to the space. The individual essentialness each member holds in the community or group is directly linked to being a valued member. The root of essentialness bridges your background and life experiences to the productive outcomes of the equity-centered community, regardless of the group's purpose.

When you are in-community and know you are valued, deficit-based language and microaggressions are not bantered around in attempts to diminish or shrink any layers of your individual dimensions of diversity. The value theme of the Belonging data set includes telltale signs such as, *Part of the bigger picture and needed. A place where you can be your best self . . . in a space that celebrates you. Knowing you can be yourself and still be loved.*

Participants' responses to What does belonging mean to you? included personal details like *accepted no matter my baggage, feeling valued*, and knowing you are *valued for who you are as a human*. Belonging calls for being fully *seen, recognized,* and *appreciated* for one's individuality. Understanding an individual's desire to *add value* to the community includes each person's inner perception of adding to the group's worthiness, independent of perceived personal flaws and others' attributes.

The personal value individuals add to equity-centered communities of belonging lives in both our heart and head. We feel and know, not just suspect, when we are valued.

Connection

Next up, a look at the final theme of the Belonging data set, *connection*. As this theme emerged, the qualitative researcher in me was giddy and filled with, what I can only describe as, a researcher's high. The reason for my giddiness and researcher's awe becomes clear in the next chapter.

Many participants' responses signaled the importance of community and connection in belonging. Statements such as *How the people around you fit into your circle of life*, *Being part of something bigger to the benefit of the individual*, and *Belonging is the certainty I am connected and an essential component of a community* indicate belonging includes being part of a larger group or collective.

Belonging data points such as *Building a community together*, *Having a voice at the table*, and *Connected* through *ownership and shared mission* point to collaborative efforts and collective efficacy work. Some responses joined the connection data theme of belonging with thoughts and feelings of connection. Responses like *A feeling of purpose* and *Being able to share what is on my mind* suggest belonging involves a sense of emotional and thoughtful connection.

When people belong, there is no pretense to blend in, no need for fitting-in masks. Belonging is *Having a voice, a purpose, and a shared mission*, and *Feeling safe (physically, emotionally) and connected*. When people know they belong, equity-centered communities are built together.

At the beginning of this chapter, you were encouraged to personally connect the Belonging data set to your life experiences. Pause and Process next; just as session attendees did, intentionally name and own your working definition of belonging below.

Pause and Process

1. How do you define Belonging? What does Belonging mean to you?
_____
_____
_____
_____
_____

2. Name a place *you know you belong*.

_____
_____
_____

3. Think of a time or circumstance when you knew you did *not belong*. Describe the circumstances, as you are able and comfortable, include your feelings, thoughts, and actions.

_____
_____
_____
_____
_____
_____
_____
_____
_____

4. Consider the four Belonging data set themes: Safety, Authenticity, Value, and Connection. Which of the four was missing from your response to #3 above, and why was the belonging element missing?

_____
_____
_____
_____
_____
_____
_____
_____
_____
_____

5. Now reflect on the place you named in #2 above. Describe how you feel and what you think as you envision yourself in that space.

_____
_____
_____
_____
_____

6. Finally, with the thoughts and feelings you identified above, how will you use those truths to interrogate the status quo in places and spaces where equity-centered communities of belonging could exist and do not? Be specific, even if you only identify the first, next step.

_____
_____
_____
_____
_____
_____
_____
_____

> **Safety + Authenticity + Value + Connection = BELONGING**

Chapter Takeaways

This chapter provides qualitative data points collected on the essentialness of Belonging. When people know they belong, there is not a need for random acts aimed at fitting in. How do you demonstrate your personal value for Belonging? What does Belonging mean to you?

Pause to reflect your personal definition of Belonging with the four qualitative data themes represented in this research:

- Safety
- Authenticity
- Value
- Connection

10 Showing Up with Hope

There is no such thing as idle hope.—Karl Menninger

Hope anchors current purpose and passion to future outcomes. Psychologically investing in the future, and understanding how goals are met with measured hope, is like making a deposit in your personal Hope Account. Respecting and holding space for your background and life experiences, while also holding tightly to your passion for the future, adds to your Hope Account. The layers of hope you *show up with* psychologically contribute to your Hope Account like Hope Dividends.

Before exploring the qualitative hope data themes, establish a mindset of either agreeing to agree or at least agreeing to meet in the moment[1] around the *possibility* of hope-filled power. Pause for an instant and consider a short-term goal you currently have. The goal might be as straightforward as planning to have your favorite meal later today, reaching out to someone you have not heard from in a while, or possibly it is a more significant goal such as initiating a courageous conversation with someone you suspect might be resistant.

Whatever goal you named, you identified your own example of a hope dividend. The seeds of hope exist in every plan and goal we name for ourselves, regardless of the magnitude or potential impact of the goal.

Hope-filled possibilities expand the parameters of options and opportunities for forward progress. "If we have goals, then hopeful thinking naturally applies" (Snyder 1994, 257). The resourcefulness of hope allows people to sustain efforts longer, hold tighter to possibilities, and try again.

The qualitative data themes for the *Hope* data set are depicted in Figure 10.1:

Resilience

Hope-filled people hold on with emotional and cognitive flexibility. The resilience theme of the Hope data is steeped in knowing every day is not

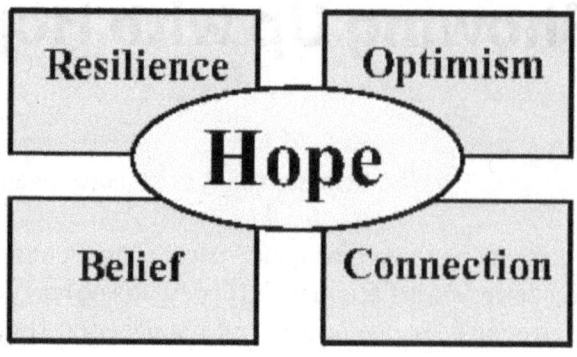

Figure 10.1 Hope data themes. Perkins (2025).

filled with all that we planned and sometimes, regardless of the amount of preparation and strategizing, goals are not met. Hope is not absent in these instances of missed opportunities. In fact, according to the data, the human characteristic of resilience is a primary component of people's hope definition because of the real possibility of failed attempts and trying again with an altered course.

The truth is, "We reinforce our capacity for hope each time we experiment with problem-solving strategies and persist until one works" (Lopez 2013, 19). Resilience is the strength of hope, not despite life difficulties, rather because life experiences are guaranteed to, at least occasionally, be completely unexpected and undesired. This data theme directly acknowledges life is challenging and complex at times. The resiliency of hope is a lifeline attached to more than one way forward.

The goal-directing and planning associated with the resilience theme of the hope data set include knowing and understanding past failure and disappointment do not diminish the possibility of the next success. In fact, responses like *the limitless possibilities in the future*, having *the faith in a possibility*, and *hope is the belief that there is a better day ahead* offer a glimpse inside the thought process of hope-filled people. Hope is *believing that something will/can happen despite other factors going against it*. Clearly, hope includes a foundational belief in the potential for positive change and improvement. Acknowledging past upsets and near-misses adds to the potency of resilience.

The resiliency of hope also includes growth, potential, and perseverance. Data points such as *no matter how hard a situation becomes you know there is a way and you continue to try and knowing it can get better* suggest hope involves strength to endure challenges and persist through adversity. Some data points highlight resilience and the ability to cope as key aspects of hope. For instance, *Hope is the ability to find the silver lining* and *Hope is the quiet, determined voice that drives my actions*. This resilience data theme is a foundational element of the failing forward mindset. "Rather than being driven by their goals, high-hope people gain satisfaction all along the journey" (Snyder 1994).

Belief

The Belief data theme is the place where Hope Dividends multiply. The undercurrent of hope-filled strength is sustained by the Belief data theme of hope. Data points such as *A belief in the world, people, and life as basically good; a belief things can improve* are examples of a disposition rooted in hope. *A belief that my part in the world matters. I believe hope is the largest picture of where we want to be, and how we want to see people succeed. It is the ultimate goal for happiness, rising above something, coming out of a tough place as a better human being, and coming together to change the world.*

Hope-filled people hold the belief, the value-centered principle, of hope. *Hope means sustaining the belief that justice, peace, and liberation are attainable.* The physiological understanding that energy is contagious to the third degree provides a springboard for those of us who have experienced the belief in hope as a shared commodity. When a hope-filled person shares the belief in the power of hope with another, the chain reaction is measurable.

Do you have any background experiences closely interacting with someone who leads with the belief of hope? And have you been a part of a team, community, or organization when the leader seemed to be missing the belief of hope? What was the effect and impact on the environment in either scenario? The Belief theme of hope is not something tangible we can hold in our hands, and yet, while there is not a physical manifestation, there is certainly a held power and benefit when belief in hope is present. Hope is *Belief with certainty. The belief that what I need and what I seek will come to fruition.*

Optimism

Hope ignites possibility. The Optimism data theme lays the groundwork for carrying mission and vision forward, even when the odds seem formidable. Responses associating hope with optimism and a positive outlook are tied to the intrinsic human understanding that regardless of the intensity of the storm, the clouds will dissipate. However, this data theme is not associated with unrealistic optimism. Snyder's (2000) findings suggest hopeful people collectively embrace optimism without harboring unrealistic levels of an optimistic approach. Hope is *knowing that even in the dark or despair, there can be a sliver of light that can grow.*

The idea of ignoring potential pitfalls is a hollow interpretation of Optimism, the forward-facing hope data theme. Not only does a high-hope person experience failure and setbacks at similar rates as others with less hope (Snyder 2000), when the inevitable setback occurs, hope-filled people understand the value of mapping an alternate plan with the newly acquired information of what did not work.

Data points such as *the possibility of something better, trust in a positive future,* and *believing that all people and systems can change for the better* suggest hope contains the building blocks of personal agency in decision-making. High hope increases personal agency.

Other data points point directly to personal disposition, Always *believe something wonderful is about to happen, Hope is knowing that I can cope today, tomorrow, and in the future, when I do not know what I will face,* and *Belief in something in the future that's better* suggest hope involves a positive outlook and *optimism for a better future if we believe in ourselves and others.*

This Optimism data theme of the hope data set suggests the internal drive derived from hope; *hope is the fire that lights the soul* and *the ability to dream.* As hope projects into tomorrow, data points reveal, *Hope is the belief that there is a better day ahead* and *believing in the possibility and creating action to support it.*

Connection

Remember in the previous chapter as the final data theme for the Belonging data set was shared and I used the word "giddy" to describe my reaction as themes emerged for both Belonging and Hope? Here is the reason—Connection emerged as a data theme, independently, from both data sets. Connection through hope is a *roadmap to achieve the impossible together*. When respondents defined and described belonging and hope individually, the conduit for both is authentic connection. Hope exists when *we are listening deeply to one another's stories, believing people's truth, and learning and becoming better humanitarians*.

The Connection data theme emerges in the hope data set as the durable driver, bringing people in equity-centered communities together expressed through data points such as *feeling connected and knowing you have something to look forward to*. The Connection data theme describes circumstances laced with promise for tomorrow, with one another. Data points such as *Hope is when the shared vision begins to grow and spread, not yet sustainable, but ready to break forth into the light* and *I believe hope is the largest picture of where we want to be, and how we want to see people succeed* tell the connection story through mission and purpose.

A deeper sense attached to hope through Connection is realized in data points such as *anticipation for an exciting event together* and *the belief that the equity work we do together today will make tomorrow better and more equitable*.

As you read the identified definitional data themes for belonging and hope, what did you notice? Which data points energized you? Are there data points you are curious about?

Apply the reflective process you practiced earlier in section one, here around belonging and hope. Connect your ideas and thoughts with the learning layers, and name your potential next steps related to hope.

Practice implementing the written reflection process leveraging the Hope data set.

> Name!
>
> Name a part (or parts) of the hope definitional data that resonates with you.
>
> _____
> _____
> _____

Connect!

Unpack and understand the connections. Use the following questions as thought builders. What are some of the existing connections to your current understanding, values, intentions? What might be a new connection or set of connections creating opportunities for deeper understanding? What are your growth implications/areas? Which part of the Hope data matters to you and/or others?

_____
_____
_____
_____
_____
_____
_____

Learn!

This section of the reflection asks and answers the four learning layers questions in relation to the topic and connections. Focus on yourself in response to each of the following:
What am I learning? Unlearning? Relearning? Resisting learning?
Reminder, this section of the reflective process specifically focuses on taking ownership of personal learning.

_____
_____
_____
_____
_____
_____
_____

Do!

This is the action phase of the reflective cycle. Consider this your fuel for hope-filled, purposeful next steps. This fourth section of the Reflective process is solidified with goal setting, including progress monitoring. Describe your next steps, consider, and name time, people, and resources. What did the Connect and Learn sections of this reflection stir within you? How will you hold yourself able, capable, and accountable?

_____
_____
_____
_____
_____
_____
_____
_____
_____
_____

When was the last time you considered the seam between your current reality and disposition to future outcomes? Hope lies in wait, just below the surface, not in frightful anticipation, rather in the optimistic truth that when you are able to think of one possible pathway, there are in fact others. Hope-filled people understand making time to invest in creating common language and shared definitions of hopeful actions matters.

How we look for hope, how we hold hope, and how hope is shared in the equity-valued communities we co-create allows us to stretch toward self-actualization, the top of Maslow's (1943, 1968) pyramid. Creating authentic communities energized by hope starts with you, or it does not.

How you *show up* in spaces, informally and formally, depends in part on the systems, policies, and practices in place *and* is nested within your purpose, passion, and community memberships. How you show *up* in spaces and places is primarily determined by Will and Skill. Understanding, and assessing individual Will and Skill, is an activity bound in courage. The heart and hard work of naming and isolating some of the obstacles facing leaders, regardless of position, who want to create systems focused on creating, sustaining hope-fill communities of equity, and belonging begins with personal reflection.

Your footing on the path toward creating and sustaining equity-centered communities of belonging is sharpened or dulled by your hold on hope. Do you have a tight grip on the strength of hope or a tenuous grasp laced with *but, what if?* How will you decrease the space between current realities and tomorrow's bold hopes? The first step, emboldened with hope, is yours to take or not to take. How bold is your hope?

> **Resilience + Belief + Optimism + Connection = HOPE**

Chapter Takeaways

Each time you intentionally invest in future goals and measure the progress toward achieving those goals, even incrementally, with hope, you are making a deposit in your personal Hope Account. The layers of hope you *show up* with increase your hope currency, like Hope Dividends.

What is your response to Connection independently emerging in both the Belonging and Hope data sets?

What personal associations do you have with the Hope data themes:

- Resilience
- Belief
- Optimism
- Connection

Note

1. Notice the omission of the offer to "agree to disagree." When people agree to disagree, the unspoken understanding is neither of us are interested in learning the other's perspective or even curious enough about one another's context for arriving at the point. I have joked, only partially, with some graduate classes the only gift I want is for people to stop taking the easy way out by agreeing to disagree. Thoughtful curiosity about how we each arrived with opposing viewpoints creates possibilities around understanding one another at a deeper level. We are agreeing to see and know each other when we meet in the moment.

11 When Belonging and Hope Coexist

The Sweet Spot of Equity-Centered Communities

When a person truly belongs, feels safe and comfortable to show up as their authentic self, embraced and able to share goals for the future, then hope and belonging create a synergistic dynamic. The combined effect of belonging and hope generates a *connection* not otherwise possible. Mutuality and humanity are grounded in the opportunity to come together, empowered for the heart and hard work of sustaining an inclusive community.

The discovery of one central data theme which created a common thread throughout the foundational elements of this work, belonging, hope, and equity-centered communities, was electrifying for me as a researcher and a seeker of individual stories. The final analysis of the large data set confirmed the grounding principle of *Connection* as a common data theme between and among the belonging and hope data sets.

Connection is the conduit of belonging and hope.

When hundreds of individuals from across the United States and international points like Australia and Canada were asked the same definitional questions about belonging and hope, as with all credible research, the results were unknown. Values and principles are relative, as life experiences and backgrounds create context on an individual basis. So, asking people from a variety of places, with a variety of lived experiences, representing a multitude of diverse dimensions, the themes were unpredictable.

As a researcher and self-proclaimed data sleuth, I mined the qualitative data focused on identifying and analyzing themes, patterns, and outliers. The fresh insights from committed individuals focusing on creating equity-centered communities of belonging and hope are firmly tethered to the power of authentic Connection (Figure 11.1). If only it were possible for me to insert a few exclamation marks following the previous sentence to emphasize the level of awe I experienced as the data analysis unfolded *with a clear throughline.* We do not need shared lived experiences to have shared goals for a better tomorrow, accomplished through the connection linking belonging and hope. The sweet spot of equity-centered communities of belonging and hope is authentic connection.

In Chapter 9, as the qualitative data was introduced, you were encouraged to notice how you personally connect the dots between the emerging data themes of belonging and hope with your lived experiences. What are your personal associations, your ah-ha's, as you read highlighted data points for belonging and hope?

What personal system of accountability will you implement to continue practicing and applying the tools in this reading? You have engaged in three intentional self-reflective practices throughout this book: Pause and Process, the Four Stages of Learning©, and a reflective cycle.

The tool(s) you choose to leverage provide an engaging, systematic self-reflection—the first step in creating equity-centered communities of belonging and hope.

Do your reflections draw from the wholeness of your lived experiences, not just the shiny parts you offer under the bright lights of your public-facing self? Notice what lingers in the shadows of your thoughts and actions as you practice self-reflection. Hold your hope closely, no matter the size, because *hope is the antidote* to real and perceived feelings of exclusion and faux inclusion. The contagion of hope is not yours to hold; spread it. "Hope cannot

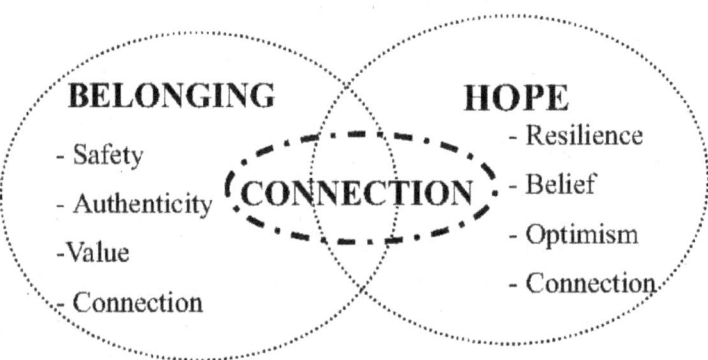

Figure 11.1 Connection is the conduit of belonging and hope. Perkins (2025).

be achieved alone. It must in some way, or another be an act of community" Lynch (1974).

The volumes of research conducted by thought leaders long before I leaned into the work point to the active elements of hope-filled, equity-centered communities of belonging. The shadows of hopelessness and exclusion are blotted out by the power of owning your story, with the same deftness of honoring others' lived experiences. My research zeroes in on the strong ties between reflection, equity-centered communities, belonging, and hope. Self-reflection purposefully creates space for you to own your personal story.

As most research about hope, this work joins a larger body of hope research, C. J. Snyder's Hope Theory (2000). Snyder devoted decades as a hope researcher and professor at the University of Kansas at Lawrence. Snyder developed and operationalized the three prongs of the Hope Theory: goals, pathways, and agency. Snyder's foundational research names hope as something learned, an active and flexible value individuals can intentionally invest in for themselves and others.

The definitional hope data gathered for this book and the four identified themes—Resilience, Belief, Optimism, and Connection—are evidence-based markers for the persistent complexities of hope people still hold today.

Cultivate the 'energy is contagious' truth, especially when feelings of powerlessness and the often-overwhelming feelings associated with defeat push to the front of your thinking and doing. My hunch, based on hundreds of conversations and personal encounters, is you can almost immediately name the place you last caught a spark of hope. Accept my would-be challenge. When you think about a spark of hope, who or what circumstance comes to mind? What energy are you carrying and spreading? Supply hope-filled energy. Look for your people, other Hope Makers; they exist.

Snyder's (1994) research details people's capability to manifest hope. When you connect with others around shared values centered on equity and vision, do not stop looking for others whose lived experiences do not match yours and yet they carry hope and equity as values. Keep going and growing the community by recognizing shared humanity, not necessarily shared experiences.

Figure 11.2 The framework for equity-centered communities of belonging and hope. Perkins (2024).

The working definition established for belonging at the opening of this book ... when people feel seen, valued, and hold essentialness within the group provides scaffolding points for Hope Makers. As clearly illustrated in the belonging and hope definitional data collected and analyzed for this work, the crossover element for each is authentic connection (see Figure 11.2). Connection, validation, and inclusion go hand in hand with the working definition of community.

The conceptual framework for this research in Figure 11.2 depicts the relationship and foundational structures of self-reflection with the tightly woven elements of community, belonging, and hope, united by connection. Self-reflection is about your personal progress. A caution-filled reminder, self-reflection is not a measure of yourself in comparison to what you deem is someone else's progress, or lack thereof. If you are spending more time charting another's progress rather than your own, it is time to adjust your focal point.

Lean into the Four Stages of Learning© specifically related to belonging and hope.

Check in with yourself in relation to the ideas and concepts you held at the outset of this reading and *where* you are now:

What are you learning about yourself?

_____
_____
_____
_____

What are you *re*learning about yourself?

_____
_____
_____
_____

What are you *un*learning about yourself?

_____
_____
_____
_____

What are you *resisting* learning about yourself?

_____
_____
_____
_____

As you engaged in the reflective processes within this book, you created personal pathways for growth. If your hope-filled goals include creating equity-centered communities of belonging, the necessary first step is self-reflection. The willingness to interrogate where you stand, how you arrived at that spot, and your next step is not sustained by happenstance; instead, the will and skill necessary to pause, process, identify personally held biases, and hold yourself accountable to lean into the Four Stages of Learning© come down to the degree of your desire to connect with others. Connection.

The research is clear: belonging and hope are fueled by the possibilities only present when authentic connection exists. The glue for creating and sustaining equity-centered communities of belonging and hope is within each of us. Choosing to stand in our individual experiences without discounting another person's or group's experiences is unifying, albeit difficult, and at times seems impossible.

How will you leverage your will and skill to plant seeds of hope? What is the next courageous conversation you will have with yourself first through reflection?

It is your story; write it well. Stay hopeful, curious, and reflective. Lean into the uncomfortable possibility of creating equity-centered communities of belonging. How will you sustain the momentum of personal and systemic growth? What is your personal fuel for the hope-filled journey?

Being just like your neighbor is not the goal; understanding and seeing your neighbor as a complex person whose life experiences and background matter and contribute as much to the story of humanity as your own is, at least, part of the goal. Personal and systemic growth are the foundational

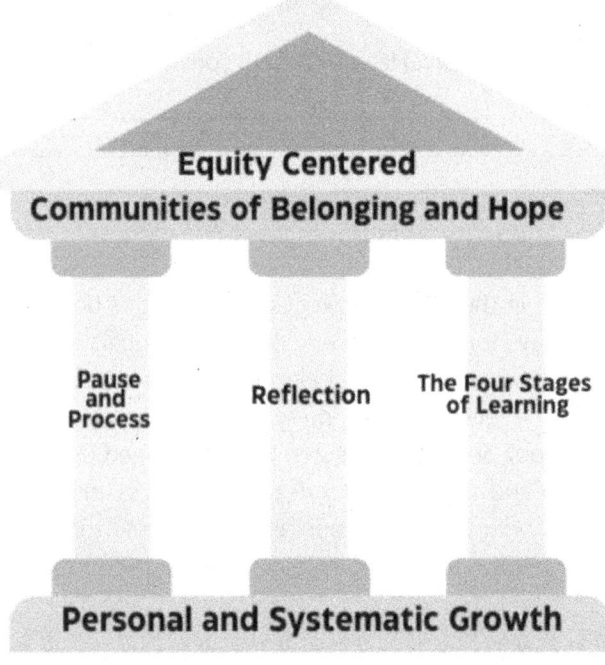

Figure 11.3 Mental model for building and supporting equity-centered communities of belonging and hope. Perkins (2024)

elements strengthened by uncovering and (re)discovering who you are as you intentionally Pause and Process, Reflect, and leverage the Four Stages of Learning©.

Figure 11.3 depicts a mental model to support your progress on the continuum of personal growth as you intentionally leverage the tools and strategies of this work. Individually, none of us have all of the answers to creating equity-centered communities of belonging and hope. Together, we hold the key.

> *Whatever the problem, the community is the answer. How we are together in our relationships is the solution.*
>
> *Margaret Wheatley*

12 Hope Anyway

> *"Revisit, reclarify, and recommit to what your soul desires."* —Susan Scott

When I began my doctoral studies as a middle school principal, whatever idealized perceptions I held prior to seeking the degree, I clearly recall waves of inadequacy rolling around at the notion of conducting my own research. There was little possibility of hiding the uncertainty I and others were experiencing when the department chair visited the Research Methodology class early in the process.

With a knowing smile, looking each one of the terrified and hopeful graduate students in the eyes, his advice was straightforward, "choose a topic you are passionate about." He continued with phrases like "a topic that matters to you," "something you *must* know more about" and with pointed emphasis, he added, "When your study is complete, you will know your research more deeply and thoroughly than anyone else." My internal processing of the message, the warning, the advice the department chair offered included the question, "What am I curious about? What do I not simply *want to* learn more about; what do I *have to* know more about?"

Fast forward to the 2020s when several times over the course of the two years I spent researching and consuming everything I could find on the topics of inclusive communities, belonging, and hope for this book, I realized I was not only researching, writing, and reporting on these topics because of the almost certain importance each holds for humanity, though that is certainly true. My reasons and natural affinity for belonging in a hope-filled, inclusive community reach far back to my childhood.

I am certainly not the first, or most talented writer and researcher on any one of the topics offered in this work. I *am* a researcher who knows firsthand about the sphere of influence self-reflection encompasses for hope-filled people—people with an internal drive who *want to and must* build equity-centered communities, not walls to divide. I am the researcher and writer who spent more than three decades keenly observing, and being simultaneously mystified and demystified, at the lengths some people choose to go to include *or* exclude others in spaces where there is most definitely room for more, not less.

I know the bold and courageous power of hope because I have witnessed, shared, and held both. I have experienced basking in the essentialness of a community *and* of being othered. My hunch is *you* have also experienced both sides of belonging and hope.

As this book moved through the publication process in late 2024, the wars around the globe, political and social unrest, and pain humans inflicted on each other were sobering, oftentimes terrifying, and certainly isolating. We do not have to look too far for examples of breaches in community standards or the divisive caverns caused by dominant cultural ways of thinking and being.

Unless and until, each of us is willing to honestly reflect on what is preventing our inclusive community building, personal and systemic biases remain intact and thriving. Name your fear, uncertainty, and confusion through the reflective cycle process; whatever you bring out from the shadows can no longer loom over your shoulder, holding you back from progress. Name your joys, successes, and celebrations as you build your reflective muscles; self-reflection is meant to capture your whole story, not just the tragedies or just the triumphs.

Investment and the active decision to know, understand, and dismantle personally held biases is the individual integrity commitment hardwired to accountability. The heart and hard work of looking for and creating equity-centered communities were started before you and me, and still, there is more to be done. Mutually agreed upon *and* upheld community values *are* sustainable, even in the inevitable disagreement.

Pause and Process

Consider recent initiatives, goals, and mandated policies and practices in your setting. Who was a part of the decision-making process, and who was not? Who was invited to participate in the decision-making process, and who decided?

_____
_____
_____
_____

1. Based on your lived experiences, what are the key elements of an inclusive community?

   _____
   _____
   _____
   _____

2. Describe your level of (dis)comfort around the pace of inclusive progress in your setting(s).

   _____
   _____
   _____
   _____

3. What are some of the barriers blocking your equity-centered, hope-filled progress?

   _____
   _____
   _____
   _____

4. Interrogate your reality, name your personal strengths, and determine what your next step(s) will be as you think about your hope-filled goals.

   _____
   _____
   _____
   _____

Sharing life experiences and background stories does not automatically create spaces laced with harmony. The ideas and topics explored in this book are not closely guarded secrets or mysterious *maybe someday* theories. Each person striving for equity-centered communities of belonging and hope, the ones brave enough to step forward, willing to own the heart and hard work of leadership, regardless of title, is indispensable.

History has shown over time that strong, equity-centered communities are not without discord. The fractures, with the potential to split wide open and divide communities, become realities when curiosity is replaced with harsh critiques and judgment. Humanity is complex. And because of the *messiness* of *being human*, tools like the Four Stages of Learning© and the reflective processes offered in this book are roadmaps for the journey. The choice of *how* we show up in a space or on a topic fraught with unconscious or implicit biases belongs to each of us. In the book *Sister Outsider*, Audre Lorde (1984) reminded us, "It is not our differences that divide us. It is our inability to recognize, accept, and celebrate those differences."

After so many years of informal and formal research for this book, I am certain: inspired, inspiring, and deliberate choices to build communities, whole communities where conditional inclusion—the great faux inclusion of humanity—does not have a foothold, happens in spaces where belonging and bold hope coexist, and where self-reflection is a desirable personal and organizational norm. When it is safe to explore personal connections and understand the origins of hidden biases, community building is possible.

It is fair to say as I began this work, and as the research continued expanding, I asked myself more times than I care to admit, "What are my contributions and how will this book add to the body of work already published on the topics?" The answers, both tangible and intangible, live within the real strategies, research, prompts, and thought threads throughout the book. Getting to the finish line was never optional for me, regardless of the self-imposed barriers. Quite simply, the results of the data collected for this book must be shared so the stories of equity-centered communities of belonging and hope continue building.

The impact and potential for forward momentum when you, a consumer of this book, lean into the power of self-reflection is limitless. There is not *a* single, secret recipe for building healthy, equity-centered communities of belonging and bold hope. The ingredients are here, as you pause and process, and investigate *where* you are in the Four Stages of Learning©, naming action-oriented calls to action for yourself.

Chapter Takeaways

Making the case for self-reflection and equity-centered communities of belonging and hope is part of what connects each of us, not despite our differences, rather, because of our individual human layers. So, make the case. Choose to walk the talk. Know *your why* before you ask others to name their why.

Reflect.

- Keep practicing.
- Keep it real.
- Keep it honest.

Then take the next, first step. Nurture belonging. Liberate hope. The path will inevitably include boulders to navigate around and bridges to cross.

Be bold enough to hope anyway.

Belonging and bold hope start with you. *You* are prepared.

Bibliography

Allen, K. A., D. L. Gray, R. F. Baumeister, et al. "The Need to Belong: A Deep Dive into the Origins, Implications, and Future of a Foundational Construct." *Educational Psychology Review* 34 (2022): 1133–56. https://doi.org/10.1007/s10648-021-09633-6.

American Library Association. "The American Library Association (ALA) champions and defends the freedom to read as promised by the First Amendment of the Constitution of the United States." 2024. https://www.ala.org/news/mediapresscenter/presskits/surge-book-challenges-press-kit.

Arriaga, Trudy T., Stacie L. Stanley, and Delores B. Lindsey. *Leading While Female: A Culturally Proficient Response for Gender Equity*. Thousand Oaks, CA: Corwin, 2020.

Arzonetti Hite, Susan, and Jenni Donohoo. *Leading Collective Efficacy: Powerful Stories of Achievement and Equity*. Thousand Oaks, CA: Corwin Press, 2021.

Baldwin, James. "As Much Truth as One Can Bear." *The New York Times*, January 14, 1962.

Baumeister, Roy F., and Mark R. Leary. "The Need to Belong: Desire for Interpersonal Attachments as a Fundamental Human Motivation." *Psychological Bulletin* 117, no. 3 (1995): 497–529.

Brown, Brené. *Atlas of the Heart: Mapping Meaningful Connection and the Language of Human Experience*. New York: Random House, 2022.

Brown, Brené. *I Thought It Was Just Me (But It Isn't): Telling the Truth About Perfectionism, Inadequacy, and Power*. New York: Gotham Books, 2007.

Brown, Brené. *The Gifts of Imperfection: Let Go of Who You Think You're Supposed to Be and Embrace Who You Are*, 10th anniversary ed. Center City, MN: Hazelden Publishing, 2021.

Channing Brown, Austin. *I'm Still Here: Black Dignity in a World Made for Whiteness*. New York: Convergent Books, 2018.

Chism, Dwayne. *Leading Your School Toward Equity: A Practical Framework for Walking the Talk*. Alexandria, VA: ASCD, 2022.

Cobb, Floyd, and John Krownapple. *Belonging Through a Culture of Dignity: The Keys to Successful Implementation*. San Diego, CA: Mimi & Todd Press, Inc, 2019.

Davis, Angela. "Public Talk on Social Justice." YouTube video, 2022. https://www.youtube.com/watch?v=BLkOLxFlcW8.

Dewey, John. *How We Think: A Restatement of the Relation of Reflective Thinking to the Educative Process*. Boston: D.C. Heath & Co Publishers, 1933.

Dweck, Carol S. *Mindset: The New Psychology of Success*. New York: Ballantine Books, 2008.

Emerson, Ralph Waldo. "Self-Reliance." In *Essays: First Series*, 52. Boston: James Munroe and Company, 1841.

Fry, Louis W. "Toward a Theory of Spiritual Leadership." *The Leadership Quarterly* 14, no. 6 (2003): 693–727. https://doi.org/10.1016/j.leaqua.2003.09.001.

Fuentes, Agustín et al. "American Association of Physical Anthropologists Statement on Race and Racism." *American Journal of Physical Anthropology* 169, no. 3 (2019): 400–2.

Glaser, Barney G., and Anselm L. Strauss. *The Discovery of Grounded Theory: Strategies for Qualitative Research*. Chicago: Aldine, 1967.

Hammond, Zaretta. *Culturally Responsive Teaching and the Brain*. Thousand Oaks, CA: Corwin, 2015.

Hooks, bell. *Teaching Community: A Pedagogy of Hope*. New York: Routledge, 2003.

Jensen, Robert. *The Heart of Whiteness: Confronting Race, Racism, and White Privilege*. San Francisco: City Lights Books, 2005.

King, Martin Luther, Jr. "Address in Washington, DC." February 1968.

Ladson-Billings, Gloria. *The Dreamkeepers: Successful Teachers of African-American Children*, 2nd ed. San Francisco: Jossey-Bass, 2009.

Lawler, Edward E. *Motivation in Work Organizations*. San Francisco: Jossey-Bass, 1994.

Lindsey, Delores B., and Randall B. Lindsey. "Build Cultural Proficiency to Ensure Equity." *Journal of Staff Development* 37, no. 1 (2016): 50–6.

Lopez, Shane J. *Making Hope Happen: Create the Future You Want for Yourself and Others*. New York: Simon & Schuster, 2013.

London, Jack. *The Call of the Wild*. New York: Macmillan, 1903.

Lorde, Audre. *Sister Outsider: Essays and Speeches*. Berkeley, CA: Crossing Press, 1984.

Love, Bettina L. 2019. *We Want to Do More Than Survive: Abolitionist Teaching and the Pursuit of Educational Freedom*. Boston: Beacon Press.

Lynch, William F. *Images of Hope*. Notre Dame, IN: University of Notre Dame Press, 1974.

Marzano, Robert J., Timothy Waters, and Brian A. McNulty. *School Leadership That Works: From Research to Results*. Alexandria, VA: ASCD, 2005.

Maslow, Abraham H. "A Theory of Human Motivation." *Psychological Review* 50, no. 4 (1943): 370–96. https://doi.org/10.1037/h0054346.

Maslow, Abraham H. *Toward a Psychology of Being*. New York: Van Nostrand, 1968.

Maxwell, John C. "What Are You Reflecting On?" *John Maxwell Blog*, 2019. Accessed 2024. https://www.johnmaxwell.com/blog/what-are-you-reflecting-on/.

McCarty, Teresa L. *Language, Literacy, and Power in Schooling*. Mahwah, NJ: Lawrence Erlbaum Associates, 2005.

McIntosh, Peggy. "White Privilege: Unpacking the Invisible Knapsack." In *Re-Visioning Family Therapy: Race, Culture, and Gender in Clinical Practice*, edited by Monica McGoldrick, 147–52. New York: Guilford Press, 1998.

Menninger, Karl. "The Academic Lecture: Hope." *American Journal of Psychiatry* 116, no. 6 (1959): 481–91.

Merriam-Webster. Accessed 2023. https://www.merriam-webster.com.

Nair, Keshavan. *A Higher Standard of Leadership: Lessons from the Life of Gandhi*. San Francisco: Berrett-Koehler, 1997.

Nicot, Jean. *Trésor de la langue française*. 1606.

Powell, John, and Stephen Menendian. "The Problem of Othering: Towards Inclusiveness and Belonging." *Othering and Belonging: Expanding the Circle of Human Concern* 2 (2016): 14–39.

Reynolds, Jason, and Ibram X. Kendi. *Stamped: Racism, Anti-Racism, and You: A Remix of the National Book Award-Winning Stamped from the Beginning*. New York: Little, Brown, 2020.

Safir, Shane, and Jamila Dugan. *Street Data: A Next-Generation Model for Equity, Pedagogy, and School Transformation*. Thousand Oaks, CA: Corwin, 2021.

Scott, Susan. *Fierce Conversations: Achieving Success at Work and in Life One Conversation at a Time*, Revised ed. New York: Penguin Books, 2017.

Seligman, Martin E. P. *Flourish: A Visionary New Understanding of Happiness and Well-Being*. New York: Atria Books, 2011.

Snyder, C. R. *Handbook of Hope: Theory, Measures, and Applications*. San Diego, CA: Academic Press, 2000.

Snyder, C. R. *The Psychology of Hope: You Can Get There from Here*. New York: Free Press, 1994.

Sotomayor, Sonia. Dissenting opinion in Schuette v. Coalition to Defend Affirmative Action, 572 U.S. 291 (2014).

Souto-Manning, Mariana, Keene, Ellin Oliver, Duke, Nell K., Martell, Jessica, Arce-Boardman, Alicia, Lugo Llerena, Carmen I., and Salas Maguire, Abigail. *No More Culturally Irrelevant Teaching*. Portsmouth, NH: Heinemann, 2018.

Strayhorn, Terrell L., and Royel M. Johnson. "Why Are All the White Students Sitting Together in College? Impact of Brown v. Board of Education on Cross-Racial Interactions among Blacks and Whites." *The Journal of Negro Education* 83, no. 3 (2014): 385–99. https://www.jstor.org.

Tuckman, Bruce W. "Bruce Tuckman's Team Development Model." 1965. https://www.lfhe.ac.uk/download.../3C6230CF-61E8-4C5E-9A0C1C81DCDEDCA2.

U.S. Supreme Court. Brown v. Board of Education, 347 U.S. 483 (1954). Washington, DC: Library of Congress.

Walton, Gregory M., and Geoffrey L. Cohen. "A Question of Belonging: Race, Social Fit, and Achievement." *Journal of Personality and Social Psychology* 92, no. 1 (2007): 82.

Wheatley, Margaret J. *Turning to One Another: Simple Conversations to Restore Hope to the Future*. San Francisco: Berrett-Koehler, 2002.

Wilkerson, Isabel. *Caste: The Origins of Our Discontents*. New York: Random House, 2020.

About the Author

Teresa Perkins, EdD, has served at every level of education for over thirty years with a mission rooted in creating and sustaining equity-centered communities of hope and belonging. A former English teacher and middle school administrator, she transitioned to higher education in 2019 at Doane University as Dept. Chair, MEd. Leadership Director, and Assistant Professor; she is currently serving as Assistant Professor in Educational Leadership at the University of Nebraska, Omaha.

Dr. Perkins presents at regional and national conferences, in addition to supporting educational and community organizations on strengthening equity-centered cultures through reflection, mission-driven decision-making, belonging, and hope.

Perkins's academic background includes earning a bachelor's degree in English and secondary education at the University of Nebraska at Lincoln, a master's degree in educational leadership at Doane University, and her doctorate degree in educational administration at the University of Nebraska at Lincoln where she was awarded the John A. Lammel Fellowship.

Above all, Teresa's most treasured times are when she is with the loves of her life—her children, grandchildren, and husband.

For speaking, consulting contact: hopeandbelong@gmail.com